INSPIRING MUSIC in WORSHIP

A short course of guided conversations for churches

Helen Bent

praxis
enriching worship today

RS✦M

Inspiring Music in Worship

Conceived and written by Helen Bent

Designed and edited by Anthony Marks

Project editor: Tim Ruffer

Editorial assistance: Dan Soper

Printed in Great Britain by Halstan & Co, Amersham

ISBN 978-0-85402-271-7

THE ROYAL SCHOOL OF CHURCH MUSIC
19 The Close, Salisbury, Wiltshire, SP1 2EB
Tel: +44 (0)1722 424848 Fax: +44 (0)1722 424849
E-mail: enquiries@rscm.com Website: www.rscm.com
Registered charity no.312828

Distributed exclusively in North America by GIA Publications Inc.
7404 S. Mason Ave., Chicago, IL 60638
Toll free: 800 442 1358
Website: www.giamusic.com

INSPIRING MUSIC in WORSHIP

Contents

Foreword

Visitors to York Minster are often surprised by the recessional singing by the choir of Psalm 150. Ironically, it is the unaccompanied singing of these words that sends a shiver down the spine, as the psalmist invites everyone to join in the worship: 'Praise him in the sound of the trumpet, praise him upon the lute and harp, praise him in cymbals and dances, praise him upon the strings and pipe, praise him on the well-tuned cymbals, praise him upon the loud cymbals. Let everything that hath breath praise the Lord!' Martin Luther said, 'Next to the Word of God, music deserves the highest praise. The gift of language combined with the gift of song was given to man that he should proclaim the Word of God through Music.'

Music itself reaches places that words and pictures cannot touch. Not only is it a language of its own, it is a whole dimension of communication. It is many languages, all at once available for the praise of God. It invites us to share both its varying moods and its capacity to interpret them. It comforts and cajoles us with both structure and freedom. To set limits on the scope of sacred music is to limit our understanding of God. St Augustine of Hippo is reputed to have said 'He who sings, prays to God twice.'

This is why I am delighted to introduce this new book from the Royal School of Church Music, designed to help churches of all kinds to engage with the breadth of the musical possibilities open to us today. It will open up a conversation that will enrich the worshipping life of our mission units. I hope that the days are gone – or soon will be – when music groups rubbish the organ as dull, or the choir dismisses the guitar or drums as unsuitable for church. Surely Psalm 150 tells us there is room in worship for a vast array of music and song?

If we have often underestimated the musicality and creativity of our congregations, we have also too often not realised how eager people actually are to engage with what worship is all about. This book will get congregations doing some theology: exploring what worship is, who it is for, and how various forms of music and song play their part. It will help church members bring out 'old treasures and new' (Matthew 13.52). It will also help churches see how sharing in music and worship will equip and inspire us day by day to join in the mission of God. And it looks fun too!

By singing the scriptures and other words of praise, we join with the angels in bearing witness to God's greatness. Somehow in singing together, filled with the Holy Spirit, we can grow in confidence to speak and sing out God's praise. Singing psalms and hymns and spiritual songs, we live the Gospel day by day, and fresh encounters with God add new dimensions to our song. We draw closer to God, and in Christ we meet the world with the full impact of God's grace and love. The Holy Spirit enables and animates our living and our worshipping, and we ourselves are changed, in St Francis' words, as we become 'instruments' of God's peace. Read this book with others, and make the most of it. 'Let everything that hath breath, praise the Lord!'

+Sentamu Eboracensis, St Cecilia's Day, 22 November 2017

Welcome to *Inspiring Music in Worship*

Inspiring Music in Worship is a course for everyone, not only musicians. Recognising that worship lies at the heart of Christian discipleship, it aims to inspire and encourage the worship of every local church. Designed to enable leaders of worship (both lay and ordained), musicians and congregations to talk to each other and reflect on worship together, its five guided conversations help to explore differences of tradition and style with honesty and respect. Everyone is invited to join in a process of exploration and discovery that makes the ongoing journey of worship into an exciting adventure.

Music forms a significant part of worship, touching depths that words alone may not. And while it is only one element among many, it is often neglected – especially by those who would not call themselves musical. This course will affirm what is good, expand our knowledge, allay our fears, and gently challenge misunderstanding and prejudice. These conversations really have the potential to revitalise the worship of local churches, providing an essential catalyst for mission and church growth.

Inspiring Music in Worship pioneers a new approach for the Royal School of Church Music, for Praxis and for the church. I have spent time listening carefully to church leaders, parish musicians and worshippers, and those outside the church. This course is a direct response to their requests and questions. It has been thoroughly trialled across England and we have found that guided conversations work! I would like to thank all those who have been involved for their commitment and careful reflection:

- Alan Mitchell, who helped to begin the process and facilitated the trial group in Rochester Diocese
- Colin Randall and Coln River Group of parishes, Gloucester Diocese
- Trial group from among authorised worship leaders in Sheffield Diocese
- Trial group from my own parish, The Rivers Team, Sheffield Diocese
- Andy Stinson, Worship and Liturgy Missioner and Rector of Barrow, Chester Diocese
- Godfrey Butland, Team Rector, Cockermouth Area Team, Carlisle Diocese
- Phil Palmer and Stephanie Tongeman, Beverley Baptist Church
- RSCM colleagues, especially Andrew Reid, Rosemary Field, Miles Quick
- Members of Praxis Council, especially Jo Spreadbury and Colin Lunt
- Anthony Marks, designer and editor, for his advice and encouragement
- Tim Ruffer, Head of Publishing, RSCM, for his advice and support
- David Bent, who has lived this project alongside me, for his helpful suggestions, his never-ending patience, love and encouragement

Helen Bent

How to use this book

A course for everyone

This course is for everyone, to help them listen to each other and listen to God afresh regarding the worship of their church. No specialist musical skill is needed. There is one book for everybody, and each participant should have their own copy. A group can be any number from two upwards, for example:

- a core worship team of ordained and lay service leaders and musicians
- a choir or music group
- a PCC
- a whole church congregation
- a team, multi-benefice, mission partnership, cluster
- an ecumenical group of churches together

Everyone has valuable experiences of worship, so everyone can contribute. There are no right or wrong answers. Every person and every church will get something different from the conversations, but in every situation those shared discussions will: deepen faith and understanding; develop shared language and promote better communication; and provide resources and tools to inspire and enhance music and worship now and in the future. The benefits of participation can be far-reaching.

One course, five sessions

The course is divided into five sessions, each with a different theme. Ideally these should run over five consecutive weeks, though fortnightly would work too. (It could be used as a Lent course.) Each session is designed to fit into two hours including a refreshment break, but the timings are only a guide. The course could run on a weekday evening, a Saturday morning or a Sunday afternoon. The most important aim is to provoke a conversation which will continue long after the course has finished.

Setting up a group

A group will need a facilitator rather than a teacher. This person need not be an expert nor need it be the vicar. Leadership of the sessions could easily be shared between group members. However someone will need to take responsibility for setting up the course and making sure the sessions happen. They will need to do the initial planning and organisation, look ahead and do any pre-session preparation. Preparation is not onerous, but may involve providing materials for group tasks and worship resources. Ideally, everyone should look ahead and get actively involved.

The group facilitator will need to be sensitive to others, recognising that worship is precious and personal to us all. Mutual respect is paramount and each person should be careful not to dominate discussions or belittle the opinions of others. Everyone needs to go away feeling that they have been heard and affirmed.

Choosing a venue

The venue will depend on the size of the group. It could be someone's home, or a room at church. Conversations work better in the round: this keeps the atmosphere informal and relaxed, and encourages collegiality. The size of the group will make a big difference to the effectiveness of discussions, so larger groups may need to be sub-divided, perhaps round tables, to make sure everyone feels able to contribute.

Format of sessions

Each session follows the same pattern; each one is presented in a different colour to aid navigation around the book. Generally the amount of time allotted to each element is the same from session to session, as shown in this plan:

Welcome and Icebreaker	15 mins
Section A	
Part 1 Guided discussion	15 mins
Part 2 What the Bible says	15 mins
Part 3 Guided discussion	15 mins
Refreshment break	15 mins

At the break, get everyone to stand up as an energy boost, even if meeting in a home. It is easy to get comfortable and let conversation and time drift. This way, there is a clear demarcation when we sit back down and continue the session. Then:

Either	
Section B (Group Task)	30 mins
or	
Section C (Case Studies)	30 mins
(except in Session 1)	
Worship	15 mins

The whole session can be held in an attitude of worship, but each one concludes with suggestions for focused worship time. After the coloured pages for each session there are supplementary materials for further thought and tasks to prepare for the next one.

Some helpful pointers

Read through each session beforehand in order to engage with the material fully. The material is self-explanatory, punctuated with questions for discussion. Conversation may be in pairs or as a group, but this is not set in stone. Use a format that works best in each situation. After the break, a group exercise and case studies offer a choice of approach, in recognition that we all learn in different ways.

How to use this book

As you go along, keep a record of any discussions, group work or practical tasks for reference and review later. This also helps to monitor how the group's thinking on worship is developing, both now and after the course has finished.

Supplementary resources are provided on-line at **www.rscm.com/IMiW** – these include further information for group facilitators, a commentary on the Bible texts, regularly updated repertoire suggestions, and links to other useful websites. See page 79 for more about training and support.

The following icons appear on the left of each page to guide you through the sessions:

 This shows the length of each activity and tracks the time within each session.

 This suggests it might be useful to make some notes to refer to later.

 This is something to think about: a pointer to direct and focus the conversation.

 This refers to Bible passages, which should be read aloud by different voices.

 This is a suggestion to discuss a topic in pairs.

 This shows you the key points to take away from each session.

 This is an invitation to discussion as a larger group.

 This is a request to think about something in your own time, between sessions.

Getting started
As we begin this exciting new venture:

- Pray for the members of the group.

- Come with an open mind.

- Come ready to give and receive.

- Come ready for a dialogue with God and with one another.

INSPIRING MUSIC in WORSHIP

Session 1

What does it mean to be a worshipping person?

Aim: to explore what worship is, and why and how we use music in worship

When in our music God is glorified,
and adoration leaves no room for pride,
it is as though the whole creation cried:
Alleluia!

Fred Pratt Green (1903 – 2000)

Session 1

Welcome
Welcome each other to this exciting adventure of discovery. Bear in mind that we are all learning together. None of us knows everything, but we can pool our knowledge and learn from one another.

Icebreaker
In pairs, think about an inspiring or significant experience of worship.

- What happened to make it so special to you?

- Why does this experience of worship stand out as memorable?

- What part did music play in this experience?

As a group
Share single words or short phrases that stand out from your conversation. You may want to jot these down to refer back to later.

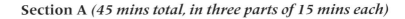

Section A *(45 mins total, in three parts of 15 mins each)*

Part 1: What do we mean by worship?
Can you define worship? It isn't easy. Some people begin with the Old English word *weorthscipe*, meaning to give worth or value to someone or something; others underline the importance of gathering for a specific time together as a congregation; whilst others emphasise lifestyle. Think about what worship means to you and make a few notes if necessary.

We could describe worship as a dialogue between God and humanity which God initiates and into which we are invited and welcomed. This ongoing conversation of God's revelation and our response will continue from now into eternity when we join with the angels and archangels and the great company of heaven. Mark Earey (*Evaluating Worship*, Grove W227, 2016) offers four different models of worship. In pairs, consider which of these models you recognise from your own experience. Could you suggest any different models?

- Worship as intimate encounter – personal with God's presence 'felt emotionally'

- Worship as edification – feeding our minds and understanding to build our faith

- Worship as duty and service – a discipline whether we feel like it or not because God is God

- Worship as ongoing offering – part of a continuous stream of worship around the world and in heaven for God's pleasure

What does it mean to be a worshipping person?

The more deeply we think about worship, the more we can see that it is complex and multi-faceted, and therefore every definition or model will limit in some way. Worship is so much more than what is said: we inhabit it and experience what is done and how it is done. It is a corporate activity of the whole people of God, bringing the church together and making it visible.

Consider too the different elements of worship. Word and sacrament, expressed through liturgy, music, prayer and action all play their part in revealing more of who God is and what God has done, and they enable us to participate and make some kind of response. Worship is an essential part of our daily discipleship. At its best, guided by the Holy Spirit, every act of worship will be unique and mysterious, giving us fresh glimpses of God.

For group discussion

- How does this relate to your own experiences of worship?

- How would you define worship?

- What helps you to connect with God and with others in worship?

Part 2: What the Bible says

- Look at the scriptures overleaf. Read each section aloud in turn.

- Leave space to reflect on any words or phrases that stand out.

- Read through all the scriptures a second time with different voices.

- Which of the texts really speaks to you? Why?

- Share your thoughts as a group. Does this look at the Bible modify your earlier thoughts about worship?

For your own notes

Session 1

The Law   **Exodus 25.1, 2, 8 NRSV**

The Lord said to Moses, 'Tell the Israelites to take for me an offering; from all whose hearts prompt them to give you shall receive the offering for me…Then have them make me a sanctuary, so that I may dwell among them.'

History   **2 Samuel 6.14, 15, 21 NIV**

David, wearing a linen ephod, danced before the Lord with all his might, while he and the entire house of Israel brought up the ark of the Lord [to Jerusalem] with shouts and the sound of trumpets…David told his wife: 'I will celebrate before the Lord.'

The Psalms   **Psalm 95.1–3, 6–8 NIV**

Come, let us sing for joy to the Lord; let us shout aloud to the Rock of our salvation. Let us come before him with thanksgiving and extol him with music and song. For the Lord is the great God, the great King above all gods…Come, let us bow down in worship, let us kneel before the Lord our Maker; for he is our God and we are the people of his pasture, the flock under his care. Today, if you hear his voice, do not harden your hearts…

The Prophets   **Isaiah 6.1–3 NRSV**

In the year that King Uzziah died, I saw the Lord sitting on a throne, high and lofty; and the hem of his robe filled the temple. Seraphs were in attendance above him; each had six wings; with two they covered their faces, with two they covered their feet, and with two they flew. And one called to another and said: 'Holy, holy, holy is the Lord God of hosts; the whole earth is full of his glory.'

The Gospels   **Matthew 26.26–30 NIV**

While they were eating, Jesus took bread, gave thanks and broke it, and gave it to his disciples, saying, 'Take and eat; this is my body.' Then he took the cup, gave thanks and offered it to them, saying, 'Drink from it, all of you. This is my blood of the covenant, which is poured out for many for the forgiveness of sins…' When they had sung a hymn, they went out to the Mount of Olives.

The Epistles   **Ephesians 5.19–20 NIV**

Speak to one another with psalms, hymns and spiritual songs. Sing and make music in your heart to the Lord, always giving thanks to God the Father for everything, in the name of the Lord Jesus Christ.

Revelation   **Revelation 7.9–10; 8.1 NIV**

After this I looked and there before me was a great multitude that no-one could count, from every nation, tribe, people and language, standing before the throne and in front of the Lamb…And they cried out in a loud voice: 'Salvation belongs to our God, who sits on the throne, and to the Lamb.'…When the Lamb opened the seventh seal, there was silence in heaven for about half an hour.

What does it mean to be a worshipping person?

Part 3: What is the place of music in all this?
Music is a means of communication and expression which crosses the bounds of age, gender, ethnicity or ability. We can all enjoy listening or joining in. Even the profoundly deaf can feel music's rhythms and vibration. Here is an opportunity to discover afresh ways in which well-chosen music can enrich the liturgy and enhance our encounter with God through Word and Sacrament.

Working in pairs, consider the role of music in worship. Is it:

- an integral part?

- a nice to have?

- an optional add-on?

- the be all and end all?

- an 'if only' on the wish list?

Which of the following statements do you think are the three most important for worship? Why? (Make a note of your answers.)

1 Music can create atmosphere and heighten liturgy and prayer.

2 Music can keep worship flowing, drawing its parts together as a coherent whole.

3 Music is able to speak to the soul without always needing words.

4 Music aids memory so that we remember words.

5 Music can enable participation by simple call and response.

6 Music can connect with the full range of human expression, emotions as well as intellect.

7 Music can be a means to unite a congregation.

8 Music has different forms and genres to be explored and savoured.

9 Music can make the liturgy stronger, especially those parts which were designed to be sung – such as Psalms.

10 Music has the power to take us beyond ourselves from present reality (immanence) towards something other-worldly (transcendence).

Share your choices as a group. You may want to record your thoughts and compare them with the words and phrases you noted down earlier.

Now take a break *(15 mins)*

Session 1

Section B *(Group task, 30 minutes)*

Be honest!
We all have our likes and dislikes in worship, especially when it comes to music. It is legitimate to have personal preferences, which may vary from day to day depending on our mood or circumstances.

On a sticky note or piece of paper, write down the names of three hymns or songs that you find particularly uplifting and helpful in worship to suit different moods. (You may want to consider times when you are happy and times when life is tough.) Then display the sticky notes or pin the pieces of paper up where everyone can see them and appreciate the range of choices. Make a note of any choices you are unfamiliar with (or take a photo of the display on your phone).

Consider the statements below. How often have you heard or said one of them, or something similar?

- 'I didn't get anything out of the worship this morning.'

- 'I don't understand why the choir needs to sing those long classical pieces that I can't join in.'

- 'I really don't like worship songs' (or Taizé chants or whatever).

- 'I can't stand all-age or baptism services, so I don't go that week.'

Working in pairs, answer the following questions:

- With which one of the statements above do you identify the most?

- Do you think we 'consume' hymns and songs to satisfy our own needs?

- How do we distinguish between valid preferences and selfishness?

- How could we be more accepting of musical taste in worship different from our own?

Now compare your answers with the rest of the group.

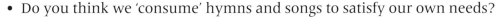

For your own notes

Reflection at the end of the day

This is adapted from a simple Examen (self-examination) in *Through All the Days of Life*, a collection of prayers compiled by Fr. Nick Schiro, S.J.

It may be helpful to light a central candle to mark a change from discussion to worship. Focus on the candle will help people to still themselves.

- **Thanksgiving**   Today, for what things am I most grateful?
    Lord, I realize that everyone, even myself, is a gift from you.

- **Examination**   Today, what have I found most difficult or challenging?
    Lord, open my eyes and ears to be more honest with myself.

- **Sorry**   Today, which of my reactions have been critical or uncaring?
    Lord, I am still learning to grow in your love.

- **Hope**   Today, how will I let you lead me to a brighter tomorrow?
    Lord, let me look with longing toward the future.

Prayer

- Pray for one another.

- Pray for the ongoing worship of your church.

- Pray for the worship life of the wider church.

Singing

Sing slowly and gently the chorus of 'Christ, be our light' by Bernadette Farrell.

Blessing

Bless one another by saying together:

> *All:* **The grace of our Lord Jesus Christ, and the love of God,
> and the fellowship of the Holy Spirit, be with us all evermore.
> Amen.**

Tips to take away from Session 1

1   Come to worship prepared to participate wholeheartedly.

2   Give glory to God and build up those who worship with you.

3   Respect worship traditions and styles different from your own.

4   Be open to learn more about God through worship whatever the style.

5   Worship is not just for Sunday – it's a way of life.

After session 1

In your own time
Look again at the list of music you and others chose in the activity at the top of page 14. Do you know all the music that others chose, or was some of it unfamiliar? Think about one of the titles listed that you don't know.

- What do you think it will sound like? Will you like it when you hear it?

- What do you think this choice says about the background or attitude to worship of the person that made it?

- Listen to some of this music if you can. Is it like you imagined?

Think back over Session 1. (You may want to look up the Bible readings and explore their context further – see the on-line resources for commentary.) Then consider the following statements. How do they relate to your worship practice?

- Worship is corporate. It is an act of giving to God to be shared with others.

- Worship is foundational. It is designed to bring glory to God and to build up the whole body of believers, growing us as disciples over time.

- Worship is missional. It is an act of proclamation declaring 'the wonders of God' to those who are not yet believers (see Acts 2.11)

Further thoughts about worship
We are all in this together, each called to be loving and to bear with one another. This demands respect for the needs and preferences of others, and generosity of attitude to those both inside and outside the church. This is wholly counter-cultural and requires us to lay down our own selfish inclinations. There is a balance between 'me' and 'not just about me'.

When we participate wholeheartedly in worship which is not to our personal taste, it may have more power because we are joining together with others in solidarity, compassion and good faith. And for those of us tempted to show off our musical talents or lord it over others as worship leaders, that focus on the almighty and the edification of others is indeed a necessary antidote to pride.

A life of worship for the whole people of God
Worship is not just about what we do on a Sunday; it is part of a greater whole. According to Romans 12: 1, we are all called to live our whole lives as an offering to God, 'a living sacrifice, holy and pleasing to God; this is true spiritual worship'. In *The Message* (Navpress, 1993), Eugene Peterson puts it another way: 'Take your everyday, ordinary life – your sleeping, eating, going-to-work, and walking-around-life – and place it before God as an offering.' This passage in Romans then goes on to talk about our role in the Body of Christ. Peterson continues: 'Each part gets its meaning from the body as a whole, not the other way around.'

Now think about your own experience of worship

- What patterns of personal worship do you follow?

- How does your personal walk with God feed into and draw from the gathered, corporate worship of the whole church?

- How might this personal and corporate worship bear witness to 'the wonders of God' to the wider community outside the church?

We are all formed by our experience of worship, alone and with others. This is a vital part of deepening spirituality and ongoing discipleship. We therefore want to encourage daily disciplines of bible reading, regular patterns of prayer and both intentional and casual listening to Christian music. We also want to spur one another on to meet for worship. Together, our own tendency to hear only what we want to hear is tempered by the contribution of others, and together, we are built up in faith and shaped into the Lord's likeness for the Lord's glory.

Preparation for Session 2: Explore your personal worship history
This exercise will enable group members to explore their personal worship history together. There are no right or wrong answers. We are who we are, with the worship experiences we have gathered over time.

Using the time-line template overleaf, note all the churches that you have attended over the years. You may also want to add in other significant worship experiences outside church, such as school assemblies and collective worship; visits to Spring Harvest or RSCM courses. Some worked examples are available on-line to give you some idea what this should look like.

You may have moved churches several times, or remained in the same church for many years. This will make a difference to your experience and what you value within worship now. Ask yourself:

- How have the traditions and styles of different churches shaped your understanding of worship?

- What kind of liturgy and music has been used?

- If you have remained in the same church over a long period, how has the worship of that church changed and developed over the years?

Bring your timeline with you to Session 2. You will be able to compare your timeline with others at the beginning of the session.

Preparation for Session 2: Personal Worship History (you may photocopy this page or download it from www.rscm.com/IMiW)

Churches where you
have worshipped

Your age	10	20	30	40	50	60	70	80	90

Other worship
experiences

INSPIRING MUSIC in WORSHIP

Session 2

Discovering skills and releasing gifts

Aim: to encourage the engagement of every
member of the congregation in worship

How often, making music, we have found
a new dimension in the world of sound,
as worship moved us to a more profound
Alleluia!

Fred Pratt Green (1903 – 2000)

Session 2

Welcome

Welcome one another back to the group and explore any further thoughts about worship which have come out of personal reflection time or further conversations between sessions.

Icebreaker

In pairs, explore your personal worship history by comparing timelines (the preparation task for Session 2 – see pages 17 and 18). Remember that there are no right or wrong answers here, only our own worship experiences. Things to consider in your conversation might be:

- Have all the churches you attended been the same denomination?
- Have all the churches been the same size?
- How have the styles of worship differed from each other?
- How did the choices or styles of music enhance the worship?

As a group

Briefly, share any significant observations which have been drawn out from the conversations. You may want to jot these down to refer back to later.

Section A *(45 mins total, in three parts of 15 mins each)*

Part 1: Worship shapes us as a community

God exists in community, one God in three persons, Father, Son and Holy Spirit, all working together and enjoying the companionship of the others. As we spend time in the presence of others, we are influenced by them and take on similar character traits. Thus, the Christian community becomes more Christ-like as it consciously seeks to spend time with God in worship, and God's living presence is made real to the participants through Word and Sacrament. Think about how the worship of your church community has shaped you and jot down a few thoughts.

Liturgy, from the Greek *leitourgia*, is defined as 'the work of the people'. This is a pertinent reminder that, as worshippers, we are all called to this together, each with an important contribution to make. We are participants not spectators. We are all invited to offer something to God and something for the benefit of one another in the church. Think about the ways in which people contribute to the worship, and compare ideas back in your pairs. (You may want to make a few notes.)

Marva Dawn remarks that 'the concept of community cannot be seen merely in terms of cosiness with God or compatibility with other members of the congregation.' She continues: 'In fact, sometimes (perhaps always?) God seems to put us in a community together with people who we don't like, so that we learn the real meaning of *agape* – that intelligent, purposeful love directed towards another's need which comes first from God and then flows through us to our neighbour.' (*A Royal "Waste" of Time*, Wm. B. Eerdmans, 1999)

It is no coincidence that St Paul wrote his famous passage about love after discussing the Body of Christ with its various Spirit-inspired gifts and before going on to talk about proper conduct in worship (see 1 Corinthians 12–14). We need each other, but we also need to understand and bear with one another's strengths and weaknesses, respecting and honouring our differences, what we simply receive from being present in worship and what we can practically offer to that worship. At best, contributions to worship will include a wide diversity of gifts – some spiritual, some practical, some more cerebral, some more creative.

For group discussion

- Do we always have to be 'active' participants or is it sufficient to contribute to worship by our presence alone?

- How might the offering of our gifts vary depending on our personal circumstances or at different stages of life?

- What kind of contributions might we be missing as a congregation?

Part 2: What the Bible says

- Look at the scriptures overleaf. Read each section aloud in turn.

- Leave space to reflect on any words or phrases that stand out.

- Read through all the scriptures a second time with different voices.

- Which of the texts really speaks to you? Why?

- Share your thoughts as a group. Does this look at the Bible modify your earlier thoughts about worship?

For your own notes

Session 2

The Law   **Numbers 8.23–26 NRSV**

The Lord spoke to Moses, saying: 'This applies to the Levites: from twenty-five years old and upward they shall begin to do duty in the service of the tent of meeting; and from the age of fifty years they shall retire from the duty of the service and serve no more. They may assist… but they shall perform no service.'

History   **1 Chronicles 15.16, 22 NIV**

David told the leaders of the Levites to appoint their kindred as singers to sing joyful songs, accompanied by musical instruments: lyres, harps and cymbals… Kenaniah the head Levite was in charge of the singing: that was his responsibility because he was skilful at it.

Psalms   **Psalm 33.1–3 NIV**

Sing joyfully to the Lord, you righteous; it is fitting for the upright to praise him. Praise the Lord with the harp; make music to him on the ten-stringed lyre. Sing to him a new song; play skilfully and shout for joy.

The Prophets   **Malachi 3.10 NIV**

'Bring the whole tithe into the storehouse, that there may be food in my house. Test me in this,' says the Lord almighty, 'and see if I will not throw open the floodgates of heaven and pour out so much blessing that you will not have room enough for it.'

The Gospels   **Matthew 25.14–18 NIV**

Jesus said: 'The kingdom of heaven will be like a man going on a journey, who called his servants and entrusted his property to them. To one he gave five talents of money, to another two talents, and to another one talent, each according to his ability…The man who had received five talents went at once and put his money to work and gained five more. So also, the one with the two talents gained two more. But the man who had received the one talent went off, dug a hole in the ground and hid his master's money.'

Acts   **Acts 2.42, 43, 46–7 NIV**

The believers devoted themselves to the apostles' teaching and to the fellowship, to the breaking of bread and to prayer. Everyone was filled with awe…Every day they continued to meet together in the temple courts. They broke bread in their homes and ate together with glad and sincere hearts, praising God and enjoying the favour of all the people.

The Epistles   **1 Corinthians 12.14, 18, 21–23, 27 NIV**

The body is not made up of one part but of many…In fact God has arranged the parts of the body, every one of them, just as he wanted them to be…The eye cannot say to the hand, 'I don't need you!' And the head cannot say to the feet, 'I don't need you!' On the contrary, those parts of the body that seem to be weaker are indispensable, and the parts we think less honourable we treat with special honour…Now you are the body of Christ and each one of you is a part of it.

Part 3: New dimensions of worship and discipleship

Methodism was said to be 'birthed in song,' making theology accessible to ordinary people and sustaining personal and corporate worship. Prompted by his conviction that singing plays a vital role in shaping the faith and discipleship of a congregation, John Wesley devised his Rules of Congregational Singing (originally printed in the preface to his *Sacred Melody or a Choice Collection of Psalm and Hymn Tunes* in 1761). Some of them are reproduced here. In pairs, work through each one and answer the questions below:

> *Rule III*   See that you join with the congregation as frequently as you can. Let not the slight degree of weakness or weariness hinder you. If this is a cross to you, take it up and you will find blessing.

> *Rule IV*   Sing lustily and with good courage. Beware of singing half dead or half asleep but lift your voice with strength ...

> *Rule V*   Sing modestly. Do not bawl so as to be heard above or distinct from the rest of the congregation that you may not destroy the harmony but strive to unite your voices together as to make one clear melodious sound ...

> *Rule VII*   Sing spiritually. Have an eye to God in every word you sing. Aim at pleasing him more than yourself, or any other creature. In order to do this attend strictly to the sense of what you sing and see that your heart is not carried away with the sound but offered to God continually; so shall your singing be such as the Lord will approve here and reward you when he cometh in the clouds of heaven.

- Which rule do you think is the most important for worship? Why?

- How do these rules fit your own experience of music and worship?

- Does your church have any rules of its own (explicit or otherwise)?

According to Karl Barth: 'The Christian church sings. It is not a choral society. Its singing is not a concert. But from inner, material necessity it sings.' (*Church Dogmatics Study Edition Vol.1*, T & T Clark International, 2010, page 240.) There is no doubt that singing has played a vital part in the life of the church over the centuries. If the community loses its ability to sing, it loses something of its heart and this needs recovering.

Share your responses to Barth as a group. You may want to record your thoughts and compare them with your earlier discussions.

Now take a break (15 mins)

Choose one of two pathways: Section B or Section C
This is an opportunity to get practical and explore ways of valuing gifts and releasing untapped resources within your church. You may wish to follow both pathways by forming two groups, one for each section; or you may prefer to focus on one. Either approach is fine.

Section B *(Group task, 30 mins)*

Everyone has a part to play
On a large piece of paper, make a list of all the members of your regular weekly congregation to see what rich resources and untapped talents are already there in the church. Alternatively, a spider diagram may be a helpful way to do this.

As a group, think about each of the age groups below. How do they contribute to worship?

- Toddlers may copy others or join in worship in their own way.

- Children may learn songs for collective worship in school. They begin to take responsibility for simple tasks within their classroom.

- Teenagers may explore the latest Christian music via social media. They may be developing musical gifts, expressive/creative arts or computer skills.

- Those aged 20–45 may have new contemporary ideas, infectious passion, energy and enthusiasm.

- Those aged 45–65 may have transferable work and life skills to offer.

- Newly retired people may have time to develop new skills.

- Older people may have liturgy and hymnody committed to memory and rich worship experiences spanning many decades.

- Unchurched newcomers may offer a fresh and questioning perspective.

Working in pairs, answer the following questions regarding your own church:

- Who does what? Who could do what?

- What rich resources do you already have?

- What can the different age groups offer to each other?

- How can you draw out the untapped talents available?

- What difference might this make to regular worship?

Now compare your answers with the rest of the group.

Discovering skills and releasing gifts

Where are the untapped resources?
For this activity, you may wish to divide into smaller groups and allocate one or two case studies to each group. Below and overleaf you will find descriptions of four very different people, each with their own issues about participation. For each one, identify their key issues and suggest a helpful way forward.

The capable musician
Peter is the head of music at the local secondary school. He is an accomplished pianist and has lots of experience of conducting choirs and orchestras at school. He has been worshipping at St Mark's for the past three years, but so far he has not offered to get involved in the music of the church. He seems to take the view that he is busy with music every day at work, so he doesn't want to do it at church as well. He has few free evenings and wants a complete break at the weekend. There is a small group of willing singers and instrumentalists at St Mark's, but they wouldn't describe themselves as musicians and they lack proper leadership.

For your own notes

Hidden talent
Sharon is a reasonably competent pianist, but she is afraid that she does not play well enough to accompany a church service. Her low self-esteem fosters the belief that she has little to offer. She can often be found playing the piano at home when people visit, and she is willing to practise. Her reluctance seems to stem from a lack of confidence rather than a lack of ability. It recently came to light that Sharon did volunteer to help during the summer holidays. One member of the congregation insensitively drew attention to a few wrong notes. Sharon has not offered since.

For your own notes

Session 2

Busy, busy, busy!

The vicar at St Giles is keen to develop the music of the church. He is aware that various young people are now learning musical instruments at school and he has spotted one girl with a lovely solo voice. He is prepared to invest time in the music to get a more orchestral-style group off the ground. He also suspects that there are some adults with rusty instrumental skills who have violins or flutes tucked away at home in the cupboard. A few people have mentioned that they would enjoy singing together but everyone is so busy and under so much pressure from exams or work, it is difficult to move things forward.

For your own notes

I can't sing!

Darren listens to all kinds of music at home and in the car. He says he's not musical because he cannot read music or play an instrument. He has always enjoyed singing from being very young, but only sings at home when he is sure that no one else can hear. He is convinced he can't sing, having been told as much by his class teacher at primary school, who didn't want him in the school choir. A new singing group has recently started at All Saints, and the choir leader is eager to draw in more male voices. Darren would really like to join this group, but he is afraid he won't be able stay in tune and may put others off.

For your own notes

 As a group, share your thoughts and insights about each of these people.

Offering ourselves and our talents to God

Mark the change from discussion to worship by laying a Bible, a hymnbook, and a musical instrument on a small central table. We may also be able to think of other things to represent the offering of ourselves and our talents to God in worship, such as a guitar plectrum or capo; a choir medal; a sketch pad; a duster; a collection plate.

Either: Choose one of the bible verses in this session as a focus

Or: Meditate on part of the Prayer of St Francis of Assisi:

> O, Divine Master, grant that I may not so much seek
> to be consoled as to console; to be understood as to understand;
> to be loved as to love; for it is in giving that we receive;
> it is in pardoning that we are pardoned;
> it is in dying that we are born again to eternal life.

Prayer

- Thank God for each member of your congregation.
- Pray for discernment regarding hidden talent.
- Pray for the people you need to enable worship to flourish.

Some suggestions for singing

- Make me a channel of your peace (Sebastian Temple)
- Brother, sister, let me serve you (Richard M. Gilllard)
- From heaven you came (The Servant King) (Graham Kendrick)
- One is the body (John Bell)

Tips to take away from Session 2

1. Honour and respect every contribution to worship.
2. Model wholehearted participation for others.
3. Rejoice in your neighbour's talents more than your own.
4. Always affirm and encourage the developing skills of others.
5. Don't underestimate the power of personal invitation.

After session 2

In your own time
Look again at the lists of people you and others created in the task on page 24. Were there any surprises or things you hadn't thought of before? Did any hidden talents emerge?

Think back over Session 2. (You may want to look up the Bible readings and explore their context further – see on-line resources for commentary.) Then think back a bit further – to the end of Session 1 and the statement on page 16:

- Worship is corporate. It is an act of giving to God to be shared with others.

What is the difference between being and doing – being with God in worship and doing for God in worship?

Further thoughts about worship
We should recognise that people come to church for many different reasons and these reasons may vary during different seasons of life. Some may not want to do anything except attend, even though options to participate more actively are offered to them. They simply want to be in God's presence and in the presence of God's worshipping people. This is perfectly valid and should be valued and affirmed.

However, this does raise questions about active and more passive participation, and the role of worship in ongoing discipleship. As we open ourselves to God in worship, we allow ourselves to be transformed in some way, becoming more like Jesus through the work of the Holy Spirit. And part of becoming more like Jesus includes serving others.

- What are our expectations of ourselves and one another?

Apprenticeship is key
We are all called to be worshippers and members of a local congregation, but our function and responsibilities will be different; for example, welcomer, service leader, preacher, musician, singer, cleaner, flower arranger, reader of scripture, intercessor, member of refreshment team: you may be able to think of others. All these roles contribute to the regular worshipping life of a church in some way, although some may be more visible than others.

In calling his disciples, Jesus gave us a fascinating model of apprenticeship. He personally invited twelve men to walk alongside him for three years. He spent quality time with them, showing them what to do, encouraging them to join in, letting them have a go themselves, allowing them to learn from their own mistakes, and then finally handing the task over for them to continue. The disciples looked far from eligible, yet Jesus trusted them to continue his mission and ministry. An apprenticeship model will help us to prepare for succession and guard against people getting stuck with the same job for life!

- How does this relate to the Bible text we read earlier about the Levites?

It takes time to apprentice others. It can be tempting and often easier to do a task ourselves rather than encouraging and training others. Sometimes we may feel threatened by the talents of others, especially when they are more gifted than we are. And sometimes we may try to cling on to power in an unhealthy way. Jesus gave us a model of servanthood, and did not see power as something to be grasped (see Philippians 2.5–11). No task was too menial for Jesus. If we serve we will reproduce, and if we reproduce we will grow the church.

For further reflection

- Who are the unlikely apprentices in the worshipping congregation?
- How will they learn and develop the skills they need?
- Who are the significant role models? Why?

Preparation for Session 3: Reflect further on the worship of your church
This exercise will enable group members to explore their church and its worship from different angles.

Try to visit the church when it is empty.

- What is the building like when it has no congregation present?
- What draws your eye and attracts your attention?
- What does this say about worship and what is important to worshippers?

Compare your thoughts with your experiences at regular services:

- What draws your eye and attracts your attention first now?
- What kind of atmosphere is being created?
- What part does the music play in this?

Now, consider how worship might be experienced by visitors:

- What might attract their attention when the church is empty?
- What might attract their attention when worship is in progress?
- What might they take away with them from the experience?

Use the table overleaf to note down your responses.

The empty church

What is the church building like when it has no congregation present?

What draws your eye and attracts your attention?

What does this say about worship and what is important to worshippers?

The church during regular worship

What draws your eye and attracts your attention first now?

What kind of atmosphere is being created?

What part does music play in this?

Worship through the eyes of visitors

What might attract their attention when the church is empty?

What might attract their attention when worship is in progress?

What might they take away with them from the experience?

INSPIRING
MUSIC in
WORSHIP

Session 3

Music and mission

Aim: to explore how inspiring worship can be
the key to effective mission

So has the church, in liturgy and song,
in faith and love, through centuries of wrong,
borne witness to the truth in every tongue:
Alleluia!

Fred Pratt Green (1903 – 2000)

Session 3

Welcome
Welcome one another. As a way of gathering everyone, why not begin this session with a hymn or song focused on mission? Suitable choices might be:

- 'We have a gospel to proclaim' (Edward J. Burns)
- 'I will sing the wondrous story' (Francis H. Rowley)
- 'Jesus, hope of the nations' (Brian Doerksen)
- 'Will you come and follow me' (John Bell and Graham Maule)

Icebreaker
In pairs, share your observations and experiences of the church empty and the church during a service (the preparation task for this session, given on page 29). Then think about an occasion when you walked into a place well out of your comfort zone for the first time and what it felt like.

- How does this relate to visitors looking around the empty church?
- How does this relate to visitors coming to a service for the first time – perhaps a baptism, wedding, funeral, or a regular weekly service?

As a group

Briefly, share any significant observations which have been drawn out from the conversations. You may want to jot these down to refer back to later.

Section A *(45 mins total, in three parts of 15 mins each)*

Part 1: Missional worship
All Christian believers are called to be disciples and every local church is called to play its part in the *missio Dei* (the mission of God). It is part of the deal. The Great Commission (Matthew 28.16–20) challenges us to go into the world to make disciples of all nations, baptising and teaching them. The Second Vatican Council puts it this way: 'The church on earth is by its very nature missionary' (David Bosch, *Transforming Mission*, 1991, page 9). Like the first disciples, we are sent out from worship to make a difference in the world. But in what sense is worship itself missional? Jot down a few ideas from your own experience.

Christian Schwarz of Natural Church Development (NCD) talks about 'inspiring' worship as one of his eight primary characteristics which help to grow the church. He is referring to an inspiredness that comes from the Spirit of God, which draws people into church irrespective of liturgical tradition or style (*NCD Handbook*, 1996). Good quality and intentionality are also cited as key factors in mission and church growth, rather than style of worship (see *From Anecdote to Evidence*, Church Growth Research Programme, 2014).

Back in your pairs, consider these discoveries further and compare them with your own findings:

- What will inspire and enable the worship and prayer of visitors in an empty church?

- What will inspire and enable the worship and prayer of visitors in a regular service?

The content of our worship will either draw people in or put them off. 'Inspiring' worship should contain profound 'So this is God!' moments, which may be converting and transforming both individually and corporately.

Worship can be a launch pad for mission. We hope to take the whole congregation, both regulars and visitors, on a journey which intentionally encourages them to engage with God and helps them grow in their understanding and discipleship. Ideally, this worship will inspire and energise regular worshippers while simultaneously welcoming strangers, offering a safe place of exploration for the searcher and a place of sanctuary for those in need or distress. Inspiring worship really is crucial to the mission of every local church.

For group discussion

- Which elements of worship inspire the congregation to grow and deepen their faith and discipleship?

- How will regular worship inspire us to 'go out and make disciples'?

- Which elements of worship might reveal something of God to newcomers to a service?

Part 2: What the Bible says

- Look at the scriptures overleaf. Read each section aloud in turn.

- Leave space to reflect on any words and phrases that stand out.

- Read through all the scriptures a second time with different voices.

- Which of the texts really speaks to you? Why?

- Share your thoughts as a group. Does this look at the Bible modify your earlier thoughts about worship?

For your own notes

Session 3

The Law   Exodus 15.1, 11, 13–14 NIV

'I will sing to the Lord, for he is highly exalted. The horse and its rider he has hurled into the sea…Who among the gods is like you, O Lord? Who is like you – majestic in holiness, awesome in glory, working wonders?…In your unfailing love you will lead the people you have redeemed. In your strength, you will guide them to your holy dwelling. The nations will hear and tremble…'

History   2 Chronicles 6.32–33 NIV

[At the dedication of the Temple] Solomon prayed: As for the foreigner who does not belong to your people Israel but has come from a distant land because of your great name and your mighty hand and your outstretched arm – when he comes and prays towards this temple, then hear from heaven, your dwelling place, and do whatever the foreigner asks of you, so that all the peoples of the earth may know your name and fear you, as do your own people Israel.

Psalms   Psalm 105.1–4 NIV

Give thanks to the Lord, call on his name; make known among the nations what he has done. Sing to him, sing praise to him; tell of all his wonderful acts. Glory in his holy name; let the hearts of those who seek the Lord rejoice. Look to the Lord and his strength; seek his face always.

The Prophets   Isaiah 61.1–3 NIV

The Spirit of the Sovereign Lord is upon me, because the Lord has anointed me to preach good news to the poor. He has sent me to bind up the broken-hearted, to proclaim freedom for the captives and release from darkness for the prisoners, to proclaim the year of the Lord's favour and the day of vengeance of our God, to comfort all who mourn, and provide for those who grieve in Zion – to bestow on them a crown of beauty instead of ashes, the oil of gladness instead of mourning, and a garment of praise instead of a spirit of despair.

The Gospels   Luke 24.28–31a NIV

As the disciples approached the village…Jesus acted as if he were going further. But they urged him strongly, 'Stay with us, for it is nearly evening; the day is almost over.' So he went in to stay with them. When he was at table with them, he took bread, gave thanks, broke it and began to give it to them. Then their eyes were opened and they recognised him…

Acts   Acts 2.1, 4–6, 11,12 NIV

When the day of Pentecost came, the believers were all together in one place… All of them were filled with the Holy Spirit and began to speak in other tongues as the Spirit enabled them. Now there were staying in Jerusalem God-fearing Jews from every nation under heaven. When they heard this sound, a crowd came together in bewilderment, because each one heard them…declaring the wonders of God in their own language. Amazed and perplexed, they asked one another, 'What does this mean?'

Music and mission

Part 3: Singing the Christian story

Pope Francis suggests that worship plays a vital part in mission: 'The Church evangelises and is herself evangelised through the beauty of the liturgy.' (*Evangelii Gaudium/The Joy of the Gospel*, 2015, Section I.24) When the beauty of the liturgy is matched with appropriate music, worship can soar, transporting the soul and acting as a window through which to glimpse the divine, maybe for the first time. But what music is appropriate to nurture the faith of the congregation and to proclaim the Christian story to unbelievers? (Make a note of some possibilities.)

Much of everyday life is accompanied by background music. In church, too, music is a significant part of worship, but here there is a difference: people are expected to join in. Visitors may have little or no knowledge of hymns or worship songs and little experience of corporate singing. They may feel awkward and reluctant to join in, so careful choice of repertoire is vital. In pairs, think back to the hymns and songs you listed in the group task in Session 1 (page 14).

- What will these songs tell the enquirer about God?

- Which songs might bring comfort or hope in times of need or sadness?

Liturgy and hymnody are both key factors in shaping faith and teaching doctrine, so it really matters what words we put on people's lips, whether said or sung. Singing inspiring words to familiar tunes can encourage visitors to engage with worship more fully. The use of well-known secular tunes to connect with people has been a part of religious music for centuries, applied by composers such as J. S. Bach (post-Reformation), the Wesleys (Methodism), William Booth (Salvation Army) and more recently John Bell (Iona Community). This practice, known as *contrafactum*, allows the substitution of a new set of words without substantially altering the existing music, working on the principle that we know what we like and we like what we know!

- Can you think of any examples of *contrafactum*?

- How do we bear witness or proclaim the gospel through our choice of music?

- How might this relate to a baptism service where the visitors greatly outnumber the regular congregation?

Share your insights as a group. You may want to record your thoughts and compare them with your earlier discussions or your discoveries in Sessions 1 and 2.

Now take a break (15 mins)

Choose one of two pathways: Section B or Section C
This is an opportunity to get practical and explore ways of connecting with the local community through worship inside and outside the church building. You may wish to follow both pathways by forming two groups, one for each section; or you may prefer to focus on one. Either approach is fine.

Section B *(Group task, 30 mins)*

Five Marks of Mission
Since 1984, 'Five Marks of Mission' have been developed and established by the Anglican Consultative Council to express the Anglican Communion's understanding of God's holistic and integral mission. There is a common commitment around the world to these marks. As a group, take each one in turn. How are their sentiments expressed within the liturgy, music, prayers, symbols or actions used in worship?

1. To proclaim the Good News of the Kingdom

2. To teach, baptise and nurture new believers

3. To respond to human need by loving service

4. To seek to transform unjust structures of society, to challenge violence of every kind and to pursue peace and reconciliation

5. To strive to safeguard the integrity of creation and sustain and renew life of earth

Now think specifically about the music used regularly in your worship.

- Can you think of hymns and songs which resonate with each mark?

- Which marks are most strongly represented in the regular music repertoire?

- Which marks are weakly represented?

- Are any marks missing all together? Why might this be the case?

Now be even more specific. For each of the five marks, make a list of hymns and songs which could be used in worship to make connections with the church's mission to the local community and wider world. The list might include familiar resources and repertoire already in regular use as well as new possibilities.

It may be helpful to refer to a selection of different hymnbooks with good biblical and thematic indexes. A comprehensive list of possibilities is provided on-line for you to refer to after the session.

How does worship connect with the community?
For this activity, you may wish to divide into smaller groups and allocate one or two case studies to each group. Below and overleaf you will find descriptions of four different opportunities to make effective links with local communities. For each one, identify the key factors involved and use this as a springboard to consider what might be appropriate to connect with people in your area.

A church-run community choir
Holy Trinity has not had a church choir for many years, but there have been repeated requests for a community choir in the area. A willing choir director from another church has been enlisted to help, and he has established a growing group of singers from church and community which meets to practise in the church. The choir is open to all. There is a growing sense of friendship and mutual support, and it is good therapy for people in high-pressure jobs and those struggling with illness or bereavement. The choir mixes popular songs and classic church music. Its 'anthem night' was a great success, and the singers are now preparing for a spring concert.

For your own notes

Church and Parish Council together
The significance of Remembrance Day in the village has been increasing. As the war memorial is a long way from the church, it has been hard to coordinate worship with the Act of Remembrance. Three years ago, St John's offered to hold the service in the community hall, which is nearer the memorial. Church and Parish Council now work together. After a short service in the hall, everyone walks to the memorial. Children from the local school come in uniform, bringing small wooden crosses which are included in the official wreath laying. With refreshments back at the hall, connections and mutual appreciation between church and community are growing.

For your own notes

Open-air worship at a community landmark

The restored flour mill is both a local tourist attraction and a working mill. A raised terrace stands above a cobbled courtyard, creating an ideal space for events. The instrument store and rehearsal room for the local brass band is located amongst the mill buildings. For several years now, the mill has hosted an annual carol service led by the brass band and singers from a Churches Together group. This year, the curator initiated a worship event in late August with a harvest theme. With echoes of Lammas (meaning 'loaf Mass'), flour from the mill was used to provide a traditional harvest loaf. The band again provided the music, which combined classic harvest hymns with more contemporary worship songs.

For your own notes

Supporting school worship

Various members of St Hilda's church are school governors. They have been keen to get involved with collective worship in school, and a small group now regularly takes part. The children also make regular visits to church for project work and for seasonal services at the end of each term. Many of the children from the monthly Messy Church are pupils at the school. As children, parents, teachers and church members get to know one another better, church and school are gradually building up a shared repertoire of music, making the children and their parents feel welcome and included whether they come to a school event or a regular church service.

For your own notes

 As a group, share your thoughts and insights. Have these case studies triggered any new ideas which could open up opportunities for the church out in your local community?

Go into all the world
Mark the change from discussion to worship by laying out symbols of the local area: photographs, a local paper, a community magazine.

Reflection
Use the photographs and symbols to help you reflect on different places in your community: shops, schools, library, doctors, community buildings, landmarks. Let these reflections lead into prayer.

Prayer

- Thank God for all your links with the local community.

- Pray for eyes to see new opportunities to worship with the community.

- Pray for worship that connects well both inside and outside the church.

Some suggestions for singing

- 'Go forth and tell' (James Seddon)

- 'God of justice' with chorus 'We must go' (Tim Hughes)

- 'Sent by the Lord am I' (Jorge Maldonado to Central American folk melody)

Sending out
To be said facing outwards towards different parts of the community

Leader   We go into the world to walk in God's light,
to rejoice in God's love and to reflect God's glory.

Leader   To a troubled world: *All*   **peace from Christ.**

Leader   To a searching world: *All*   **love from Christ.**

Leader   To a waiting world: *All*   **hope from Christ.**

All   **We go into the world to walk in God's light,
to rejoice in God's love and to reflect God's glory.**

Tips to take away from Session 3

1   Determine to integrate worship and mission more effectively.

2   Aim for inspiring worship which draws people in 'all by itself'.

3   Be as welcoming and as inclusive as possible.

4   Be authentic – people are looking for the 'real deal'.

5   Leave people with food for thought, wanting to come back for more.

After session 3

In your own time
Look back to Session 1, which reminded us that worship is not just about what we do during a service in church (see page 16). We are sent out from worship to actively engage in God's mission but we are also called to a worship lifestyle, inside and outside the church building. Both bear witness to the Kingdom of God and our calling to follow Jesus. So, in the broadest sense, how missional is our worship?

- How will newcomers feel welcomed and accepted by God?

- How will newcomers learn more about what God is like and what the Christian life is about?

- What will make them want to come back again and discover more?

- What role does the Holy Spirit play in inspiring worship which will connect and draw people in 'all by itself'?

Think back over Session 3. (You may want to look up the Bible readings and explore their context further – see the on-line resources for commentary.) Then consider how we might sing the Christian story in a relevant way to connect with our present context.

- How might our worship become more intentionally mission-shaped?

- What role can seasonal services play in singing the story?

Further thoughts about worship
When music and worship are fully integrated into a church's mission and outreach, there is no doubt that they generate great potential to grow that church. A breadth of accessible, well-chosen hymns and songs really does make a difference, although we may lose something of the beauty and richness, awe and mystery if we always go for the simple and accessible.

A hundred years ago, we would have found broadly similar music being used in most churches in the UK, probably involving an organ, a choir and hymns sung by the congregation, although before that the village band would have been the norm, and there were periods when no instruments were used at all. Since the 1960s, we have seen a vast increase in choices and diversity of musical styles using a range of instrumental resources.

Cultural change
Our present culture has gradually lost any real sense of shared, corporate song. Technology has furthered this consumer culture in which personal taste has become dominant. Now that each person can create individual play-lists on computer, tablet or phone, listening is often mediated through headphones,

so that the experience remains individual and is not shared corporately with others. Our taste becomes ever more refined as we select our favourite tracks, mixing and matching rather than playing through whole albums.

At the same time, far fewer people make their own music at home and we have become accustomed to a level of professionalism and musical excellence in recorded music which has left many volunteer church musicians looking no more than enthusiastic amateurs. Perhaps we should value amateurs more highly – they willingly give their best for the love of what they do, rather than financial reward.

However, technology may also have opened up new avenues for us. Backing tracks on CD or mp3 enable churches and schools alike to accompany communal singing when they have no musicians; recorded music also opens up the possibility of including other music of different styles and genres from contemporary secular to classical. Video recordings of live performances with attractive graphics and lyrics on media sites take this a stage further.

- How might contemporary secular music be used to bring people into the presence of God?

We might legitimately argue that three of the five Marks of Mission (see page 36) are humanitarian in ethos rather than specifically Christian, but Jesus made it quite clear he had come to minister to the widow, the orphan, and the misfits and outcasts of society. We need to remember that we receive many newcomers to church through times of difficulty or bereavement.

For further reflection:

- How do we welcome the stranger, particularly the marginalized and those of different ethnicity: migrants, refugees or asylum seekers?

- What music might include and encourage people to join in?

- What music might exclude and shut people out?

Preparation for Session 4: Explore and research
It is very easy to make assumptions about people both inside and outside the church and their responses to the church and its worship. The only way to discover what they really think is to ask them.

To do this, use the table overleaf. Have a conversation with three people in your church, preferably one from each row (type of church attendance) and each column (age group). The questions below the table may help you to start the conversation. Use the table to jot down your findings.

Preparation for Session 4: Explore and research (you may photocopy this page, or download it from www.rscm.com/IMiW)

Type of church attendance	Age 18–40	Age 41–65	Age 66+
Regular member (someone who has been involved in worship for a long time)			
Fringe member (someone new to church for whom worship is also new)			
Non-member (someone in the community who does not come to church)			

What is it about a church service that most helps you to worship God?

In what ways does worship help you to grow in your faith?

In what ways does the music help or hinder the way you engage with God?

Where do you think the worship of the church fits into the life of the local community?

What kind of services (or worship) would you like to come to?

INSPIRING MUSIC in WORSHIP

Session 4

Starting from where we are

Aim: to evaluate our current worship in terms of genre, skill and engagement with God

And did not Jesus sing a psalm that night
When utmost evil strove against the Light?
Then let us sing, for whom he won the fight:
Alleluia!

Fred Pratt Green (1903 – 2000)

Session 4

Welcome

Welcome one another with thankfulness for the first three sessions. In the light of all the conversations so far, it is now time to look at our current worship practice honestly. We all have to start from where we are, and this will be different for each congregation.

Icebreaker

As a result of the research task on page 42, you will have had conversations with between one and three people, ranging in age and their experience of church and its worship. In pairs, share your discoveries. Consider:

- What surprised you or challenged your previous assumptions?

- How were the conversations affected by the age of the participants?

As a group

Briefly, share any significant observations which have been drawn out from the conversations. You may want to jot these down to refer back to later.

Section A (45 mins total, in three parts of 15 mins each)

Part 1: Inviting God to join the conversation

As we review our worship and its music, it is vital to listen to our regular church members, those on the fringe and ideally those outside the church too. We also need to open our ears and hearts to God. Why not pause for a moment's silent prayer: 'May we learn to see things as God sees them.'

A good way to keep God at the centre of our thinking is to look specifically at Jesus, his words and his actions.

Jesus, an example to follow

Jesus grew up within the Jewish worship tradition, which was passed down orally from generation to generation. He regularly participated in worship at the local synagogue or travelled to Jerusalem for seasonal festivals at the Temple. Jesus said nothing about music in worship, but he would have been used to singing psalms and would have known them by heart from childhood. Much of Jesus's adult ministry took place in the context of worship, often upsetting the status quo and challenging an outward show of piety in favour of sincere devotion, heart-felt prayer and radical action. How does this make you feel? Can you think of examples from the Gospels to share in your pairs?

Servanthood was also a hallmark of Jesus's earthly life, laying aside his deity, ministering with compassion to others, and eventually suffering death on the cross for the sake of humanity. Jesus made it clear to both his disciples and the crowds: 'If any want to become my followers, let them deny themselves and take up their cross and follow me. For those who want to save their life will lose it, and those who lose their life for my sake, and for the sake of the gospel, will save it.' (Mark 8.34–35)

We must recognise that any review will almost certainly result in change and that this change may be costly. It may involve us laying down our personal preferences for the sake of others and the long-term health of the church. If we cling relentlessly to a preferred tradition or style, we may be in danger of losing them altogether as congregation numbers dwindle and, at its most extreme, a service or church is faced with closure. However, when we are prepared to 'let go and let God' we are often surprised by the outcome, which may bring enrichment we didn't expect and more gains than losses in time.

For group discussion

- What would Jesus do with the worship in your church?
- How would you plan next Sunday morning differently if you knew Jesus was the guest preacher?
- How can we keep God at the centre of our worship?

Part 2: What the Bible says

- Look at the scriptures overleaf. Read each section aloud in turn.
- Leave space to reflect on any words and phrases that stand out.
- Read through all the scriptures a second time with different voices.
- Which of the texts really speaks to you? Why?
- Share your thoughts as a group. Does this look at the Bible modify your earlier thoughts about worship?

For your own notes

Session 4

The Law   Deuteronomy 6.4–7 NIV

Hear, O Israel: The Lord our God, the Lord is one. Love the Lord your God with all your heart, with all your soul and with all your strength. These commandments that I give you today are to be upon your hearts. Impress them on your children. Talk about them when you sit at home and when you walk along the road.

History   1 Chronicles 16.7–11, 36 NRSV

Then David first appointed the singing of praises to the Lord by Asaph and his kindred. 'O give thanks to the Lord, call on his name, make known his deeds among the peoples. Sing to him, sing praises to him, tell of all his wonderful works. Glory in his holy name; let the hearts of those who seek the Lord rejoice. Seek the Lord, and his strength, seek his presence continually…' Then all the people said 'Amen!' and praised the Lord.

Psalms   Psalm 92.1–4 NIV

It is good to praise the Lord and make music to your name, O Most High, to proclaim your love in the morning and your faithfulness at night, to the music of the ten-stringed lyre and the melody of the harp. For you make me glad by your deeds, O Lord; I sing for joy at the work of your hands.

The Prophets   Amos 5.21–24 NIV

The Lord says: 'I hate, I despise your religious feasts; I cannot stand your assemblies. Even though you bring me burnt offerings and grain offerings, I will not accept them…Away with the noise of your songs! I will not listen to the music of your harps. But let justice roll on like a river, righteousness like a never-failing stream.'

The Gospels   John 4.21–24 NRSV

[Speaking to the Samaritan woman at the well] Jesus said: 'Believe me, the hour is coming when you will worship the Father neither on this mountain nor in Jerusalem. You worship what you do not know, we worship what we know, for salvation is from the Jews. But the hour is coming, and is now here, when true worshippers will worship the Father in spirit and truth, for the Father seeks such as these to worship him. God is spirit, and those who worship him must worship in spirit and truth.'

The Epistles   Hebrews 10.23–25 NIV

Let us hold unswervingly to the hope we profess, for he who promised is faithful. And let us consider how we may spur one another on towards love and good deeds. Let us not give up meeting together, as some are in the habit of doing, but let us encourage one another – and all the more as you see the Day approaching.

Revelation   Revelation 2.3–5 NIV

[Written to the church in Ephesus] You have persevered and have endured hardships for my name, and have not grown weary. Yet I hold this against you: You have forsaken your first love. Remember the height from which you have fallen! Repent and do the things you did at first.

Part 3: Explore and embrace musical diversity

The Bible presents a creative tension between God who is the same yesterday, today and forever (Hebrews 13.8) and God who is always doing new things (Isaiah 43.19). Viewed positively, the push and pull between tradition in tension with current culture and the full range of contemporary church music provides fertile ground for creativity while still keeping us rooted in our Christian heritage. Each new move of God prompts a flourish of fresh creativity, appropriate to the moment. Over time this is whittled down by its quality and popular usage until only a small core remains. We have a few ancient treasures, for example:

- Hymn: 'Hail, gladdening light,' 4th century or earlier

- Plainsong: 'Come, Holy Ghost, our souls inspire,' 8th or 9th century

- Secular melody: the 'Passion Chorale': for his St Matthew Passion (c.1727), Bach harmonised the tune of a well-known love song

A change of tune and style may radically change the way we engage with a text, offering a fresh alternative for some, making it more accessible for others. Here are some recent examples of well-loved hymns presented in different ways:

- Change of mood through change of tune: 'What a friend we have in Jesus' by Joseph M. Scriven (c. 1855) set by John Bell in 1987 to the folk tune 'Scarlet Ribbons'

- Original verses with an additional refrain: 'Amazing grace' by John Newton (1772) with the refrain 'My chains are gone' by Chris Tomlin and Louie Giglio (2006)

- New verses with original refrain: Horatio Spafford's refrain 'It is well with my soul' (1876) re-worked by Matt and Beth Redman (2015)

Working in pairs, can you think of any other examples? Then consider:

- How do we balance 'the God who is the same, yesterday, today and forever' with 'the God who is always doing new things'?

Within the worship of a mixed economy church, it is easy to end up with a blend of musical styles and genres that pleases no one; but we must not assume there is no bridge between traditional and contemporary worship. There is inspiring and uplifting worship music in a wide range of genres. Some of it is lasting, some short-lived. Both can be useful, though not everything will be of equal value.

- How do we tell the 'good' from the 'bad' with integrity and objectivity?

- How might we expand our repertoire and why might this be useful?

Now take a break (15 mins)

Session 4

Choose one of two pathways: Section B or Section C
This is an opportunity to get practical and explore the strengths and weaknesses of our worship and some of the pastoral dilemmas which often face the local church. You may wish to follow both pathways by forming two groups, one for each section; or you may prefer to focus on one. Either approach is fine.

Section B *(Group task, 30 mins)*

Assessing where we are: Envelope exercise

This exercise will help us to work out more specifically where we are now in our worship, and to assess its present strengths and weaknesses. This may help us to recognise our comfort zones or where we may be stuck in a bit of a rut, while at the same time revealing new possibilities and new ways of doing things.

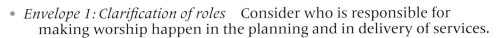

Before the session, label four large envelopes, each with one of the categories listed below. Make and distribute some blank slips of paper in two colours – enough to allow participants to put multiple slips into each envelope. Assign one colour to 'strengths' and the other to 'weaknesses'. During the session, each participant should consider each theme in turn, write their thoughts on the appropriate coloured slips, and place them in the relevant envelope. In this way, everyone can contribute freely and anonymously.

- *Envelope 1: Clarification of roles*   Consider who is responsible for making worship happen in the planning and in delivery of services.

- *Envelope 2: Communication*   Consider when and where worship is discussed, and by whom, on a week to week basis and in relation to ongoing vision and strategy.

- *Envelope 3: Practical Organisation*   Consider what has to be done to make worship happen – beforehand, on the day, behind the scenes or up front.

- *Envelope 4: Participation of others*   Consider how the congregation can get involved and make an active contribution to worship.

When everyone has finished, take Envelope 1, sort the slips into strengths and weaknesses. Then try to sort them into categories to see if any patterns or specific issues emerge. Then repeat the process with envelopes 2, 3 and 4.

Note: this exercise is too important to rush. If you need to spend the full 30 minutes filling the envelopes and run out of time, ask one person to take the envelopes away, type up their contents, and circulate round the group. This will help everyone to consider the strengths and weaknesses carefully before they give feedback. We will refer back to this exercise in Session 5.

Section C *(Case studies, 30 mins)*

What are the pastoral dilemmas we face?
For this activity, you may wish to divide into smaller groups and allocate one or two cases studies to each group. Below and overleaf you will find descriptions of four very different situations which are all commonly encountered by churches. For each one, identify the key factors involved and suggest some pastorally sensitive ways of resolving these dilemmas.

The last-minute vicar

The vicar of St Philip's has a reputation for last minute inspiration. Having chosen the music for a service well in advance, he frequently wants to change one of the hymns or songs a few minutes before the service. One of the regular musicians is a good sight reader and can handle this. However, Jane, who also plays regularly, really needs a whole week to practise. If last minute changes are made Jane gets flustered and makes lots of mistakes – even in hymns she knows well. The congregation then makes critical comments at the end of the service and Jane is left exposed and humiliated.

For your own notes

The elderly organist

George has played the organ at St Mary's for 60 years. A willing and able musician, happy to play a wide range of church music, he is now 83 years old. He is very deaf and increasingly frail. Tucked away in the organ loft, he doesn't always hear the hymn announced, so there can be long pauses. Sometimes he plays too slowly, or loses track of the verses, playing one too many or one too few. The congregation are fond of George and don't want to upset him. They realise that playing for services is a vital part of his worship and gives him a sense of value and purpose. However, his playing is becoming embarrassing and a stumbling block to mission.

For your own notes

Session 4

Us and them

Two groups are involved in worship at St Oswald's: a robed choir of long standing and a recently formed music group. The two groups view each other with suspicion, although a few people are members of both. The organist and choir are upset that the music group never seems to practise, and consider them musically inferior. The choir and organist spend a long time practising, but with dwindling numbers they seem unaware that they are not as strong as they once were. The music group actually contains competent musicians who play well together. The choir complain about worship songs with trite words sung in unison, while the music group protest over dreary, inflexible, outdated hymns. The tension is noticeable on Sunday morning when each group has its own slot in the service.

For your own notes

Put on a pedestal

David has grown up in the church: his musical abilities have been encouraged and nurtured by music group and congregation alike. Through his teens and into his early twenties, he has become an accomplished guitarist and worship leader, regularly choosing and leading worship songs in services. He has enjoyed the limelight and been put on a pedestal by others. However, his choice of repertoire is limited to the songs he likes and can play well. He leads in a particular style which others find difficult to follow. Now the church wants to broaden its worship in new directions, but David is adamant that his way is the right way, if not the only way, to worship.

For your own notes

 As a group, share your thoughts and insights about each of these situations.

Come, Holy Spirit!

Mark the change from discussion to worship by encouraging everyone to quieten their thoughts and silently ask for the Holy Spirit's guidance. Light a central candle if that is helpful, but aim for simplicity with no other distractions.

Singing

Sing the Taizé chant *Veni Sancte Spiritus* by Jacques Berthier.

Meditation

Use these words from the Methodist Covenant Prayer, taken from The Covenant Service, *The Methodist Worship Book*, 1999

> I am no longer my own, but yours.
> Put me to what you will, rank me with whom you will.
> Put me to doing, put me to suffering.
> Let me be employed for you, or laid aside for you;
> exalted for you, or brought low for you.
>
> Let me be full, let me be empty,
> let me have all things, let me have nothing.
> I freely and gladly yield all things
> to your pleasure and disposal.
>
> And now, O glorious and blessed God, Father, Son, and Holy Spirit,
> you are mine and I am yours, so be it.
> And the Covenant which I have made on earth, let it be ratified in heaven.
> Amen.

Prayer

- Ask God to help you lay aside any prejudice or fear of change.

- Pray for good communication and deeper understanding.

- Pray for courage to embrace a broader worship for the sake of others.

Tips to take away from Session 4

1. 'You are what you do, not what you say you'll do.' (Carl Jung)

2. To become more like Jesus will involve a cost.

3. To grow means to change.

4. Develop a 'have a go,' 'can do' mentality.

5. With God everything is possible.

After session 4

In your own time
Think again about your own experience of worship in the light of what you have discussed over the past four weeks.

In a fast-paced, ever-changing world, some people may seek refuge in church. This may lead to a fear of church changing and a desire to maintain things as they are 'now and for ever'. You may want to ask yourself if you are frightened of change. If so, why? What might help you to be less fearful?

For others, the grass may seem greener elsewhere and they will be eager for change. Some may be tempted to emulate worship experienced elsewhere, such as 'New Wine', 'Taizé', 'Iona', or cathedral, especially if blessed with able musicians. But the local church is not any of these things, nor should it aspire to be. We can learn from them, but we will always need to discover the authentic expression of worship for our own context. We want to value and affirm gifts, but we may also need to gently challenge prima donnas, worship leaders with inflated egos, professionalism, elitism, or anything else that may move the focus away from God onto the musicians or the quality of performance.

How might we ensure that the worship we offer

- values its heritage and remains open to new possibilities?
- is musically the best we can make it without falling into the temptations outlined above?

Think back over Session 4. Look back at any notes you made. (You may want to look up the Bible readings and explore their context further – see the on-line resources for commentary.)

If you did the envelope exercise, you may want to reflect further. Consider:

- *Envelope 1* Where does the power lie and can it be abused?
- *Envelope 2* When does communication falter and could it be improved?
- *Envelope 3* How can practical skills be developed and honed?
- *Envelope 4* What kind of congregational involvement could be encouraged in the future?

Living organisms change as they grow
We may genuinely long for our church to grow, but this will inevitably come at a cost and require change in many areas of church life. We cannot grow younger as a congregation without young families with potentially noisy children. We cannot have accessible worship without modifying our style and repertoire.

Prune for growth

As Jesus prepares his disciples for the future, he tells them 'I am the true vine, and my Father is the gardener. He cuts off every branch in me that bears no fruit, while every branch that does bear fruit he prunes so that it will be even more fruitful.' (John 15.1–2)

We are part of God's church. As members of the local 'vine', we do not have sole ownership. The Father is the master gardener and pruning is essential. If we fail to prune, a previously fruitful plant may produce branches that break under the weight of fruit. If we fail to cut back a struggling plant, it may simply not have the strength to sustain itself. By contrast, careful pruning, though painful at the time, will stimulate healthy and vigorous growth.

For further reflection

- Where is God in all this?

- What changes of liturgy or music might be required? Does this also require a change of attitude?

- What are the implications for our present or future congregations?

Preparation for Session 5: Compile a hymn and song selector list

This task will help the group to evaluate objectively the music currently being used in the church. There are no right or wrong answers, but this gives you an opportunity to compare and analyse concrete lists from each person.

Using the chart overleaf, make a list of core repertoire or what you think are the most popular twenty hymns and songs in regular use at your church at the moment. Note that this list should be jotted down quickly to help us recognise those songs that come to mind first. When you have compiled your list, consider:

- Are the choices all in the same genre? Hymns? Worship songs? Taizé?

- What are the words about? God-focused? Me-centred? Praise? Lament? Story-telling? Doctrine? Mission?

- What might be missing?

You may also want to go back to those people you spoke to before Session 4. How many hymns and songs from your list do they know? What additional hymns and songs would they want to add to the list? And what about those people outside the church? This is a good opportunity to ask them and find out what, if any, hymns and songs they already know.

Bring your list to Session 5 to compare with other people's lists.

Preparation for Session 5: A hymn and song list (you may photocopy this page, or download it from www.rscm.com/IMiW)

Title of song or hymn	Genre/style/remarks

Title of song or hymn	Genre/style/remarks

INSPIRING MUSIC in WORSHIP

Session 5

Setting a new vision for music and worship

Aim: to dream dreams and put them into action

Let every instrument be tuned for praise!
Let all rejoice who have a voice to raise!
And may God give us faith to sing always:
Alleluia!

Fred Pratt Green (1903 – 2000)

Session 5

Welcome
Welcome each other to this final session. Use a large piece of paper and some big pens to create a 'Wall of Worship'. As everyone arrives, they are invited to write down words or short phrases of worship; words of praise; cries of lament; or expressions of devotion. Why not use a line from a hymn or song?

Icebreaker
In pairs, briefly reflect on the Wall of Worship. Do any contributions surprise you? Then think back over the discussions of the past four sessions. New understanding, awareness and appreciation will have grown. In the light of this:

- What is the best thing about the worship in your church?

- What is the best thing about the music in your church?

- If you could make one change, what might it be?

As a group
Briefly, share any significant observations which have been drawn out from the conversations. You may want to jot these down to refer back to later.

Section A *(45 mins total, in three parts of 15 mins each)*

Part 1: Inspiring new vision for music and worship
Worship is living and active: there is no such thing as 'ordinary' time. Each act of worship is a unique opportunity to meet with God and one another. At the same time, many of us value the stability and predictability of familiar liturgy and music. The idea of setting new vision can be unsettling or even threatening but if we carry on as we are, we may miss opportunities to rebuild, restore and renew.

The DNA of worship
Now may be a good time to reconsider the essentials of worship, and what we think is of central importance to the worship of our church. Our DNA, carrying all the genetic instructions for life, is unique and identifies us as who we are. So how does this relate to the worship of our church? In pairs, consider:

- What is the DNA of our worship? And does that worship provide the essentials for a healthy church, including growth (mission), development (discipleship) and reproduction (making new disciples)?

- Or put another way, if local church worship was a stick of rock, what would be written right through it?

If you did the envelope task from Session 4 (see page 48), it may be helpful to add the results into the discussion at this point, to rejoice in the strengths and highlight areas of weakness that will need further attention.

Setting a new vision for music and worship

Setting vision

The writer of Proverbs tells us: 'without a vision, the people perish' (Proverbs 29.18, KJV). The Hebrew word used here for 'vision' also means insight or revelation as well as implying the need to dream dreams. *The Message* translation gives other helpful insights: 'If people can't see what God is doing, they stumble all over themselves; but when they attend to what God reveals, they are most blessed.' And we would all like to be blessed!

In worship, there are riches old and new to be savoured, but there is a tension here. Indeed worship is full of tensions as we try to balance a godly focus with the nurture of a congregation; traditional formality with cultural informality; and liturgical structure with the more free-flowing. It is wise to be circumspect so that we don't abandon our heritage or simply latch onto the latest fashion. Yet we do not want to limit God's vision, so we should not be afraid to innovate. We want to nurture faith alongside the mentality to give the new a try.

For group discussion

- What is an authentic worship style for your church? What is real for you?

- What is the prevailing attitude? Survival mode? Maintenance of the status quo? Excited at new possibilities and potential? Other?

- How can you prepare people well for trying new things in worship?

- What styles of worship will aid your church in healthy growth, development and reproduction?

Part 2: What the Bible says

- Look at the scriptures overleaf. Read each section aloud in turn.

- Leave space to reflect on any words and phrases that stand out.

- Read through all the scriptures a second time with different voices.

- Which of the texts really speaks to you? Why?

- Share your thoughts as a group. Does this look at the Bible modify your earlier thoughts about worship?

For your own notes

Session 5

The Law   **Deuteronomy 30.11, 14, 16 NIV**

Now what I am commanding you today is not too difficult for you or beyond your reach...No, the word is very near you; it is in your mouth and in your heart so that you may obey it...For I command you today to love the Lord your God, to walk in his ways, and to keep his commands, decrees and laws; then you will live and increase, and the Lord will bless you in the land you are entering to possess.

History   **Ezra 3.10–12 NIV**

When the builders laid the foundation of the temple of the Lord, the priests in their vestments and with trumpets, and the Levites (the sons of Asaph) with cymbals, took their places to praise the Lord...With praise and thanksgiving they sang to the Lord: 'He is good; his love to Israel endures for ever.' And all the people gave a great shout of praise to the Lord, because the foundation of the house of the Lord was laid. But many of the older priests and Levites and family heads, who had seen the former temple wept aloud...while many others shouted for joy.

Psalms   **Psalm 149.1, 3–5 NIV**

Praise the Lord. Sing to the Lord a new song, his praise in the assembly of the saints...Let them praise his name with dancing and make music to him with tambourine and harp. For the Lord takes delight in his people; he crowns the humble with salvation. Let the saints rejoice in this honour and sing for joy on their beds.

The Prophets   **Jeremiah 7.1–3, 5, 7 NIV**

The word came to Jeremiah from the Lord: 'Stand at the gate of the Lord's house and there proclaim this message: "Hear the word of the Lord, all you people of Judah who come through these gates to worship the Lord. The Lord Almighty, the God of Israel, says: Reform your ways and your actions...and deal with each other justly...and I will let you live in this place, in the land I gave to your forefathers for ever and ever..."'

The Gospels   **Luke 21.1–4 NIV**

As he looked up, Jesus saw the rich putting their gifts into the temple treasury. He also saw a poor widow put in two very small copper coins. 'I tell you the truth,' he said, 'this poor widow has put in more than all the others. All these people gave their gifts from their wealth; but she out of her poverty put in all she had to live on.'

The Epistles   **Hebrews 12.22–23a, 28–29 NIV**

You have come to Mount Zion, to the heavenly Jerusalem, the city of the living God. You have come to thousands upon thousands of angels in joyful assembly, to the church of the firstborn, whose names are written in heaven...Therefore, since we are receiving a kingdom that cannot be shaken, let us be thankful, and so worship God acceptably in reverence and awe, for our 'God is a consuming fire.'

Revelation   **Revelation 5.13–14 NIV**

Then I heard every creature in heaven and on earth and under the earth and in the sea, and all that is in them, singing: 'To the one seated on the throne and to the Lamb be blessing and honour and glory and might, forever and ever!' The four living creatures said, 'Amen!'. And the elders fell down and worshipped.

Setting a new vision for music and worship

Part 3: 'We are an Easter people and Alleluia is our song!'
This phrase, attributed to St Augustine of Hippo, reminds us we are an Easter people all year round. Therefore, our worship should always direct us to the joy of resurrection, and beyond to the hope of our final destination among the worshippers of heaven. What a glorious diversity we will experience in that great crowd of witnesses from every nation, tribe and language! What is your immediate response to the idea of worship in heaven? Jot down your thoughts.

Writing to the Colossian church, Paul told them to 'let the Word of Christ dwell in them richly' – not only in teaching but also as they sang 'psalms, hymns and spiritual songs ... to God.' (Colossians 3:16) Paul expected the Word of God and essence of Christian belief to be carried by song lyrics.

In pairs, look back at the hymn and song lists compiled before Session 5 (see page 54). Compare them, noting any overlaps and differences. It is all too easy to assume that 'everyone knows this, because I know it,' or that everyone knows it to the same tune. And there is a tendency in all of us to choose our favourites.

- How well do these choices reflect Paul's instruction to use psalms, hymns and spiritual songs?

- What do these three categories offer to the worshipper?

- How can we ensure a balanced diet for the congregation?

If our psalm, hymn and song repertoire depends largely on styles inherited from the past or choices of particular individuals (such as the vicar, worship leader or organist), then there may be no considered corporate input or critique.

Now share these insights with the wider group. This will help us to assess what we value and what is missing, and to see if we are stuck in a time-warp, or favour particular genres and styles at the expense of others. Ideally, we should aim for a truly representative core repertoire which everyone knows and owns. As we journey onwards together, consider:

- Do we 'consume' hymns and songs rather than live in and through them?

- How can we savour and refresh the best of the old while at the same time discerning and adding the best of the new?

- How will we continue to refresh worship regularly in the future?

Note: At the end of this session, ask one person to collate everyone's hymn and song selector lists for further consideration.

Now take a break (15 mins)

Session 5

Choose one of two pathways: Section B or Section C

This is an opportunity to get practical and explore some realistic and manageable changes that could make a significant difference to the worship of the church. You may wish to follow both pathways by forming two groups, one for each section; or you may prefer to focus on one. Either approach is fine.

Section B *(Group task, 30 mins)*

A present-day parable

Standing on the Round Tower in Old Portsmouth, there is an uninterrupted view of the ferries going out to sea. All the ferries travel out of the harbour along the same deep water channel. It is only when they get further out to sea that it becomes clear that they are going to different destinations. Some turn quickly towards the Isle of Wight, whilst others continue onwards. As they head further out, the trajectories begin to change and it becomes clear that one ferry is sailing to Cherbourg, one to Caen, one to St Malo, one to Le Havre and others to Santander or Bilbao. These significant changes of direction are achieved by very small adjustments to the wheel.

This parable can be a real encouragement to us. Vision and growth in the local church are often more about step-by-step progression than grand visions for major reform.

Working in pairs, answer the following questions regarding your own church:

- What is the direction of travel for the worship of your church?
- What do you see as your church's destination?
- Where would you like worship to be in: one year? five years? ten years?

Now compare your answers with the rest of the group. Then consider:

- What small adjustments might change your direction?
- When and how might you make these adjustments?

For your own notes

Setting a new vision for music and worship

 Small changes can make a big difference
For this activity, you may wish to divide into smaller groups and allocate one or two cases studies to each group. Below and overleaf you will find descriptions of four different situations in which small changes could make a big difference. For each one, identify the key issues and suggest a constructive way forward.

No longer set in stone
St Wilfred's has recently undergone a church re-ordering. Pews have been replaced with tasteful, flexible seating, enabling new possibilities for experimentation with café-style services and Messy Church. Space has been opened up in the chancel, but the music group are reluctant to move there in case they become a distraction. The keyboard remains where it has always been and the musicians still occupy a cramped space beside the pulpit, where it is hard to maintain eye contact with one another and impossible to see the service leader. If the music group moved into the chancel, there would be space by the pulpit for a prayer corner with votive candles.

For your own notes

The ultimate multi-tasker
Emily is a stalwart of St Peter's. Involved in the church since childhood, she is fully committed to its ministry and mission. An enthusiast and a passionate 'people' person, she seems to know everything and everybody in the congregation and community. Having raised a family of three while working full-time, she knows how to multi-task. She is a regular member of the welcome team and a communion assistant. These roles often conflict with her turn in the music group, and other group members are becoming frustrated. Emily is also on the coffee rota once a month, so on those Sundays she leaves the music group before the final hymn.

For your own notes

A church tidy up

St Anne's has a sizeable gated porch, which is always open to the public. Over the years, it has become a dumping ground for all sorts of bits and pieces from flower-stands to forgotten umbrellas. John and Sarah have recently cleared out the porch and transformed it into an attractive prayer space using a different theme each month. Church members and visitors alike appreciate this gentle welcome and introduction to prayer. John and Sarah are also members of the choir. They have now suggested a clear out of the music cupboard. Much of the music is dilapidated and smells musty, having not been used for years. Certain members of the choir are horrified. They worry that their heritage may be carelessly discarded and lost.

For your own notes

Gratitude or grumbles?

Gavin has been playing the organ and piano at St George's for several years now. He is young, competent and enthusiastic. He has recently taken part in a worship training course and has brought back some new musical resources. He has gently and sensitively tried out one or two new hymns and songs, which have been met with a mixed reception. Jean and her friends nearly always complain about something – the music was too fast or too slow, too soft or too loud. Now they have started complaining about anything new or different. The vicar is distressed by their ungrateful attitude. He appreciates Gavin's efforts but he is aware that Gavin is getting worn down by the negative response and beginning to lose heart.

For your own notes

 As a group, share your thoughts and insights about each of these situations and suggest a small change that might make a big difference.

Renewing our vision
Mark the change from discussion to worship by focusing on the idea of setting sail. You may wish to use a photograph or painting of the sea to aid reflection.

Meditation
Use the following prayer. This is frequently attributed to Sir Francis Drake as he set sail on his voyage of exploration.

> Disturb us, Lord, when we are too well pleased with ourselves,
> when our dreams have come true because we have dreamed too little,
> when we arrive safely because we have sailed too close to the shore.
>
> Disturb us, Lord, when with the abundance of things we possess,
> we have lost our thirst for the waters of life;
> when having fallen in love with life, we have ceased to dream of eternity;
> when in our efforts to build a new earth,
> we have allowed our vision of the new heaven to dim.
>
> Disturb us, Lord, to dare more boldly,
> to venture on wider seas where storms will show your mastery,
> where losing sight of land, we shall find the stars;
> we ask you to push back the horizons of our hopes;
> and to push into the future in strength, courage, hope and love.

Prayer

- Thank God for all you have shared together in the past weeks.

- Pray for wisdom to discern the way forward.

- Pray for the boldness to take the next step.

Singing
Sing *Be Thou my vision* (Irish 8th century) to encourage you on your journey.

Tips to take away from Session 5

1 Develop an attitude of thankfulness and openness to fresh vision.

2 Dare to dream dreams and never limit what God can do.

3 Savour the best of the old and discover the best of the new.

4 One small change can make a big difference over time.

5 Our final destination is the worship of heaven.

After session 5

In your own time
Look again at the hymn and song selector lists you and others made.

- How many people chose the same hymns and songs?

- How many hymns and songs featured on only one person's list?

If the church keeps records of music for copyright purposes, go through all the hymns and songs in the last year and list the twenty most frequently sung. If you are involved in different churches within a multi-benefice or circuit, it would be helpful to collate the lists church by church. This will then allow for careful comparison, noting local nuances in repertoire and style. Such lists could be really useful during a vacancy or for incoming ministers or musicians.

You may also want to compare the results more widely. A quick internet search will take you to the latest top twenty lists from Church Copyright Licencing International and other organisations.

- What hymns and songs are popular in other churches? Locally? Abroad?

- What are the implications for churches working together ecumenically?

Think back over Session 5. Look back at any notes you made. (You may want to look up the Bible readings and explore their context further – see on-line resources for commentary.)

We know worship needs to move forward and develop if our churches are to grow but our present congregations may be frightened of or resistant to change.

- Why are we so keen to stay in our comfort zone?

- What small adjustments might make a big difference in our church?

- How could we become more willing to learn new hymns and songs?

Then consider all five sessions as a whole:

- What have you personally gained from taking part?

- What might you do differently as a result?

- What might the church do differently as a result?

Further thoughts about worship: Vision and growth step by step

Vision does not always have to be grand and large scale. We have seen that small changes can make a significant difference to the direction of travel. Some small adjustments can be very practical. Here are a few suggestions to consider:

- Make the worship space more welcoming and reverential.
- Refresh tired service booklets to bring new inspiration.
- Commit to learn a new hymn or song per month.
- Spend more time preparing the content of worship.
- Develop a lay worship team that includes musicians.
- Have a meal with the musician(s) to thank, affirm and encourage them.

These small but significant steps can be achievable in any church.

From here to eternity

It is also worth remembering that not only is worship part of life on earth now – it is also preparation for heaven in the future. Worship is one of the only activities of the church which will last into eternity. The worship of heaven is our ultimate destination.

Time and again, God invites us to draw closer, reminding us what an awesome privilege we share with angels and archangels and all the company of heaven. Francis Pott encapsulates so much when he writes of 'Angel-voices ever singing round thy throne of light'. The hymn goes on to speak of 'craftsman's art and music's measure' combining for God's pleasure. In our churches, we are encouraged to use all the talents with which God has blessed us to offer 'hearts and minds and hands and voices in our choicest psalmody'. Finally, Pott reminds us that this is all about God and his 'honour, glory, might and merit' as earth and heaven come together to give their best in worship.

May we all determine to play our part in preparing for the worship of heaven where we will one day join together with the whole company of saints on earth and in heaven uttering ceaseless 'Alleluias'!

Next steps

After the five sessions
We have had some good times talking together and have now completed the course, but we cannot simply close the book and think 'Job done; mission accomplished!' It is important to end any venture well, but in reality this is not the end at all. We want to continue the conversations to help us shape our worship and use of music in the future. The outcomes will be different for every church, depending on local context. They will involve putting our learning into practice.

A key recommendation: why not have a meal together?
Once the course is completed, a shared meal in a relaxed, informal atmosphere can be a great way to thank one another for being part of the group: it also provides an appropriate moment to review and reflect once more.

Some practical suggestions

- Reflect back over the five sessions: what has really stood out?

- Revisit the results of the exercises and tasks in each session to draw out key findings. Did any issues keep coming up week after week?

- Re-consider the case studies: which ones particularly resonate?

- From your findings, create a document to summarise key areas where adjustment to music and worship may be needed.

- Give a presentation of your findings to your church.

- Check back through the tips to take away at the end of each session.

- Re-iterate the importance of a 'can do' or 'let's give this a go' mentality.

The one crucial adjustment
As a group, identify the one crucial decision that, as a result of these conversations, will be made collectively as a church regarding music and worship. Write it in the box below.

We will do this even if we do little else!

In the future

Going further

When planning the direction of travel for the future, it is important to be intentional with a clear destination in mind. This will require continuing conversations, corporate prayer, and discernment, if the vision for inspiring music in worship is going to be truly owned by the whole congregation. Any vision should reflect the needs of the present congregation but also consider the future.

Some simple strategies

- Continue to meet regularly as a group once a month or once a quarter.
- Commit to keeping the conversations going.
- Commit to developing repertoire and using music more creatively.
- Continue to develop the hymn and song selector list (see page 54).
- Invite fringe members and newcomers to the conversation.
- Use the final sections of this book to deepen knowledge and understanding, and get some practical ideas.

Other considerations to keep in mind

- Where would we like music and worship to be in:

    one year?   five years?   ten years?

- What decisions do we need to take to make this happen?
- How and when might we implement change?
- How will we keep everyone on side?

Stepping stones not millstones!

The most important things to remember are:

- Continue the conversation that has begun and build on it.
- Move forward one step at a time.
- Refresh worship regularly so we don't get stuck in a new rut!

For your own notes

FAQs: Music in worship

This part of the book offers practical help by addressing a range of FAQs: questions frequently asked by churches on a range of related music and worship topics. The conversations generated by the course itself may already have answered some of these; but here you will also find additional help and advice about how to arrive at solutions in the future by means of experiment and experience in a local context.

Our worship feels stuck in a rut. How do we use music to help us move on?

- Vary the type of music as people arrive to create a different atmosphere to lead into a service: a solo instrument or singer; organ; choir singing Taizé; music group leading up-tempo worship songs; silence.

- Experiment with alternative musical settings to refresh the liturgy, particularly for the Eucharist.

- Intentionally broaden the repertoire with some contemporary hymns and songs.

- Use an instrumental or orchestral piece from time to time to aid reflection.

For reminders about ways in which music can connect, see Session 1 (page 13). For more about where to find music resources, see pages 72–73.

How can we make better use of music in worship when there is so much choice?
Often what is needed is a better knowledge of the music available and where to find it, rather than a vastly expanded repertoire. This is where a hymn and song selector list (see page 54) can be a real asset. To get to know a broader repertoire well:

- Start with regular needs, then seasonal, then specific.

- Go for a breadth of genres to meet different tastes and needs.

- Choose hymns and songs with meaningful lyrics and strong melodies.

- Visit other churches to hear what they are singing.

- Check out top twenty lists on key websites (see page 64).

Who should be responsible for choosing the music and does it matter?
This differs from church to church and may vary from week to week, depending on who is leading services. In some cases the minister will choose all the music; in others, this will done by the musician(s). Music may be chosen in blocks a month at a time, or decided week by week. While we each have our own preferred ways of working and favourite choices, remember the aim is to enable corporate rather than individual worship (see Session 1, pages 16–17 for more).

Choosing music is a joy for some, for others a challenge. In a way, it does not matter who chooses but generally the content of worship is ultimately the minister's responsibility. A wise minister will work with others to draw out the best possibilities.

FAQs: Music in worship

How much should those responsible for the music liaise with a service leader or preacher?
The majority of people see music as an integral part of worship, but if there is little conversation between preacher, service leader and musicians, music may end up as a 'slot-filler' or an optional add-on (see Session 1, page 13). The more time we invest in planning together, the more we will understand each other and understand the intention for each particular service. Collaboration and communication will enable worship to come together as a coherent whole with clear direction and flow.

How do we choose music that is appropriate for its worship context?
Look for music that will aid memory, shape faith and grow disciples. Consider:

- The area (who lives there? who comes to church? how many members are regulars, visitors, teenagers, children? what is happening in the life of the community at the moment?)

- The type of service (Eucharist; Morning or Evening Prayer; Service of the Word; all-age; baptism, wedding or funeral; liturgical or free)

- The musicians available for that act of worship (see page 74 for more)

If large numbers of visitors are present, they may not know any church music; or they may not know your particular repertoire. On these occasions, choose congregational hymns and songs with strong melodies: a repeated refrain may help, and words that clearly communicate the Christian message. See Session 3 (page 35) for more advice.

We may have just the right choice of music, but without the musicians or singers who can lead it well, it will fall flat. If the service or sermon would really lose something without that particular piece of music, try using a professional recording of it instead.

How do we balance music with other elements of the service?
Music should enhance worship without dominating. The amount of music may vary depending on both the type and length of service, and whether liturgy is sung or spoken. If parts of the liturgy are sung, who are they sung by? Give the congregation the opportunity to join in: they may feel disenfranchised if they have to listen to the choir for too long or cannot join in with the worship band. Here are a few tips:

- When planning music, look at a running order of the service to get an overview. Look for direction and flow through the whole service.

- Compare the number of musical elements with the non-musical. Allow rests and pauses for prayer and reflection.

- Time hymns and songs beforehand – they often take longer than we think.

- Omit verses from long hymns rather than using them in their entirety.

- Balance the musical diet over time. Review repertoire every six months to see what has been heavily used and whether there are any gaps.

FAQs: Repertoire

How do we ensure that the music we choose is suitable for its position within the service?
Whatever else, the first hymn or song should gather and prepare people. Similarly, the final hymn or song should draw the act of worship to a close and send the congregation back out into the world. In between there will be other choices:

- related to the Word of God and our openness to hear it and receive it

- linked to theme, season or sermon

- related to the prayers (and may indeed be prayers set to music)

- related to the Eucharist, enabling the bread and wine to be brought forward and the preparation of the Holy Table

What is the difference between a psalm, a hymn, and a spiritual song?

Psalms:

- are Israel's songs from the Bible, which Jesus himself would have used

- connect with our emotions through praise and lament

- can be sung in a huge range of styles: plainsong; chant; metrical; responsorial; worship songs with paraphrased words

Hymns:

- have an unchanging set structure, divided into verses of equal length

- are rhythmically straightforward with a regular metre and rhyming scheme

- tell us theological or doctrinal truths through proclamation and devotion

- are usually in four part harmony, often with organ or piano accompaniment

Spiritual songs
These have a range of forms, including: anthems, solo songs, chants, raps, worship songs. Recently, however, the term spiritual songs has primarily become associated with worship songs. These:

- have a flexible structure, often using forms from pop and rock music

- have a strong underlying beat but may be rhythmically complex

- may not have a set beginning or end, leaving this up to the musicians

- are often addressed directly to God, though may still contain biblical truths

- are designed to be led by guitar and other rhythm instruments, though may include a piano part used as a guide for improvisation or embellishment

How often should we introduce new repertoire? Are there good ways to do this?
There are two opposite dangers here. Not enough change, and music may become boring; too much change and nothing is properly learned or established. Here are some hints to help you get the balance right:

- Try to plan for everyone – musicians and congregation alike – to learn new music on a regular basis, either during the service or at a specific time.

- One new hymn or song in a service is usually enough.

- Organist, choir or music group must learn new pieces very well before they are tried with the congregation.

- Subtly introduce a new piece to the congregation by playing it before a service or during communion for a few weeks: it will then feel familiar when they learn to sing it.

- Specifically teach new material to the congregation so that they learn it well: ask them to listen carefully first (without singing); work line by line, pointing out any pitfalls in the melody and correcting any mistakes.

- Use new repertoire often so that it becomes embedded: regular use will encourage familiarity and spiritual ownership by the congregation.

How do we bridge the gap between traditional and contemporary worship repertoire?
The use of these descriptions may itself be part of the problem, creating a false polarity among musicians and congregation between implicitly 'old-fashioned' hymns and 'up-to-date' worship songs. It may help to try to avoid making this distinction too strictly, and instead just consider the breadth of available repertoire, old and new. 'Traditional' can imply conservative but also suggests long-established and orthodox. In contrast, contemporary simply means 'occurring in the present time'. Therefore, contemporary repertoire is much broader than the genre of worship songs, including classical forms as well as more popular styles.

Recently, we have seen a flurry of older hymns reworked in a more popular style. See Session 4 (page 47) for some suggestions. To bridge the gap, we need to avoid the tensions and go for some easy wins:

- Choose songs that are more hymn-like in form – for congregational use, these work better than those written for lead singer and backing group.

- Beware of tricky syncopated rhythms – congregations may iron out rhythmic intricacies to make songs more singable *en masse*, or just feel unable to join in.

- Look for words that fit well in every verse or section – irregular poetry can be hard to fit to the music, making it difficult for a congregation to keep together and sing with confidence.

FAQs: Resources

How and where do we find good music resources?
Browsing online or in a Christian bookshop will reveal many possibilities, covering a range of hymns, psalms and spiritual songs. Many reputable publishers now collect a rich diversity of material old and new within one book. These also include a selection of short chants and prayer responses as well as songs from the world church. Members of the congregation may also be a good 'resource'. They may come to you with their own suggestions, having heard and used songs elsewhere.

Consider too how we define 'good'. Music dates quickly. If we introduce new material, we want it to be well received by musicians, singers and congregation alike, and to stand the test of time. Also note that not all popular, well used hymns and songs are of good quality. Sometimes they remain in use because we can find no suitable alternative. Continue to reflect on the questions in Session 4 at the foot of page 47.

How do we choose a new hymnbook?
Some hymnbooks belong to particular traditions or denominations: others take a deliberately broader or ecumenical approach. If we decide we are a certain type of church, and choose to use a particular hymnbook and no other, we may be limiting possibilities for growth and development. Try to cast your net widely when choosing. Whatever your cultural, liturgical and financial considerations, a twenty-first century hymnbook should be at least some of the following:

- Flexible, with a breadth of quality repertoire for a mixed economy church

- Wisely arranged (seasonal; thematic; liturgical; alphabetical) and well indexed so that you can access the material from different perspectives

- Written in good contemporary language, and set to familiar tunes

- Sensibly updated to make them more inclusive

- Based on good theology and sound doctrine

- Available digitally (perhaps with MIDI or audio files for accompaniments and optional instrumental parts)

- Musically versatile (key; pitch; harmonization; instrumentation; difficulty)

Think too about the practical aspects of any new resource:

- Legibility: can it be easily read by everyone in the congregation?

- Durability: is it robust enough to withstand long-term use?

- Size and weight: will everyone in the congregation be able to hold it?

- Flexibility: does it come in different formats to suit different readers (for example, text only; text and melody line; large-print)?

- Sustainability: will it remain available for a long time?

Are online resources better than printed ones?
They are different. Hymnbooks can be a good way of introducing new material as all the resource is already available in one place. But some musicians prefer to read on a tablet rather than from a book. Online resources have the advantage that we can download the music we want, when we want it, in the key we want it, at a modest cost. In the long run, this can be more economical in terms of expense and shelf-space. But books feel more solid and reliable to many people, especially those wary of technology – and to some, a 'real' book is a physical symbol of financial, emotional and spiritual investment.

Do we need to bother about copyright?
Yes! Copyright concerns intellectual property and fair payment of composers, authors and others. If you copy, print, project, download, perform, record or play recorded music in your church, there may be copyright issues. If you are in doubt about whether you need permission or a licence to use music in services or other church contexts, take advice. Information is available from a number of sources, including:

- The RSCM

- Christian Copyright Licence International (CCLI), which 'makes creative works available and licensing simple, legal and affordable'

- Decani Calamus Licence, which 'gives access to a large part of the repertoire used particularly, but not exclusively, in Catholic liturgy today'. (Calamus can also provide a separate licence for Taizé material.)

- The Performing Right Society (PRS) – chiefly for non-worship usage

How do we evaluate our repertoire and resource choices?
This course emphasizes the need for continual reflection and review of worship, so it is important to make sure this actually happens. We usually know only too quickly when a new hymn or song has not gone down well, but it is equally important to recognize that a good reception is not always a sign of a quality piece: the quality of worship may be a better indicator (there is more about this in Session 4, pages 47 and 52.) When evaluating choices, bear in mind that:

- Repetition and familiarity are key factors – it can be difficult to enter into worship with new material, but even something we initially disliked will gradually grow on us over time.

- There is a fine line between comfort and complacency – while it is good for music to be familiar, change and variety will refresh our worship and can help us to engage in new ways.

- Things we like are not always good for us – a balanced diet is essential.

- Choices do not exist in isolation and corporate worship is more important than personal taste.

FAQs: Practical music strategies

On these pages you will find some help and advice about specific music issues. (Bear in mind that further support is always available from the RSCM education team.)

I'm not musical. Who can I turn to for help with music in church?
This course has underlined the value of investment in conversation and collaboration. Ministers may lack musical knowledge or awareness of musicians' limitations, while musicians may not understand liturgical purpose or mission priority. By talking honestly, both parties can each support and educate each other and grow in knowledge and understanding. If there are no musicians available in your church, musicians from other churches in the deanery or circuit may be able to help.

Where do we find a breadth of suitable material which all the musicians can manage?
Whatever the style, music should be done as well as possible to facilitate worship, but it is not always readily transferable from organ to guitar or vice versa. In order to match repertoire choices to available musicians, it is important to remember the strengths and weaknesses of different singers and players. Here are some tips:

Classically-trained musicians:

- tend to be proficient sight-readers and play exactly what is on the page (so are accurate and reliable, but may play less 'freely' and be less adaptable)

- rely heavily on a full piano copy or given four-part harmony

- will pride themselves on precise, consistent performances

- may be challenged by the syncopated rhythms of pop and jazz

- may struggle to transpose music to a more suitable key without preparation

Pop and rock musicians:

- often play by ear and have a flexible approach to structure, chords and rhythm

- may play from chord sheets rather than standard notation (so may be less 'precise' because of the vagaries of memory)

- may value spontaneity, adaptability and unpredictability

- may feel rhythms innately and be used to both vocal and instrumental improvisation, 'making it up as they go along'

- be comfortable transposing chord-based music into more suitable keys

The organist and choir won't do worship songs!
This attitude may not be deliberate. Classically trained organists may struggle with popular styles, which often simply do not work on the organ. Singers from the choral tradition may have difficulty achieving the sound and feel of pop and rock music, which require techniques and approaches very different from the classical tradition.

However, whatever our background and ability, with a little honesty and humility we can all learn, improve and hone new skills. A few helpful strategies might be:

- Find worship songs in versions for choir and organ or keyboard – these are a good way to get more formally trained musicians used to the genre.

- Encourage singers to use their choral skills aurally to improvise harmonies they can hear (this is a challenge, but one that can be very enjoyable).

- Think of novel ways to incorporate the choir and organ within your worship songs (this involves the different parties talking to each other!).

Our choir is shrinking! What do we do?
Choirs decline for a variety of reasons. Long-term commitment can be too much for busy people. We should be good stewards of our musical heritage, but should acknowledge too that a shrinking choir will not be able to sing the same repertoire as effectively. This realisation can lead to new creative and imaginative possibilities:

- Use the choir less frequently so that singers can commit more time to fewer rehearsals and services, and find other solutions for 'non-choir' services.

- Grow a 'festal' choir for specific celebrations like Christmas or Easter.

- Invite singers from other local churches to take part in larger choral works.

- Choose repertoire appropriate to the size of choir now.

- Encourage choir members to give a lead from within the congregation.

- Use the choir as a missional opportunity, broadening its remit to include other singers from the community (see the first case study in Session 3).

What do we do with a viola and a tuba if that is all we have?
Use them! Work with the resources you have rather than those you would like. If you have one or two instruments which would not normally be found playing together regularly, apply some simple rules of arranging and orchestration:

- Go for contrast. Not everyone has to play everything: find opportunities to maximise the effect of each instrument by using them sparingly.

- Use different instruments for particular verses to enhance words, then bring everyone together for a last hymn or final verse.

- Encourage learners to play and develop their skills, but make sure these contributions are valued by the congregation and that mistakes do not become a cause for criticism or embarrassment.

- Remember that many publishers provide instrumental parts of varying levels to suit all kinds of players; if you have instrumentalists, it is worth considering this factor when selecting repertoire.

Music and theology

Since we began this course, we have achieved a great deal already. We have new plans and possibilities for the future. However, the outcomes will be even more effective if they are underpinned by a sound theological perspective to deepen our understanding of music in worship further. Here are a few pointers:

Music in worship
Although worship can happen without it, music usually has a significant part to play. Music can really help worship take off. Music, like worship, is difficult to define; yet we all know what the word means. It is an experience common to all, throughout the world. We recognise music in sounds and rhythms of nature as well as those of human making. Music is a creative and expressive art with its origins in a creative God.

Made in the image of God
As part of God's creation, we too have our origins in God. We can all appreciate music in its various forms through listening, singing, clapping along, or tapping a foot. We may hear cries of 'I can't sing' or 'I can't read music' or 'I can't play an instrument', but in fact we all have the ability to take part in some way. Thus, a piece of music becomes a dynamic, living, breathing act. Some will emulate God's creativity further with their ability to write lyrics or compose music. Christian history has affirmed music as part of the 'good' created order and a vital part of worship.

God, the singer
The prophet Zephaniah tells us that God 'will quiet us with his love, and rejoice over us with singing' (Zephaniah 3.17). We each have a voice unique to us, and we sing because God sings. We can sing for our own benefit or for the benefit of others, whether within a congregation or to quiet a fretful child with love. Singing is physically and emotionally good for us, bringing release and restoration. What is more, singing has the power to draw together and unite a random group of people into one body, reflecting the Trinity, the three-in-one God who dwells in community.

Music in the Bible
Music is present from Genesis to Revelation, and is used throughout to celebrate key moments: creation (stars and angels, Job 38.7); Exodus (song of Moses and Miriam, Exodus 15); birth of Christ (angels, Luke 2.14); resurrection (trumpets, 1 Corinthians 15.52); heavenly worship (whole company, Revelation 4, 5, 7). Singing was a key activity of God's people in worship and the Psalms formed Israel's hymnbook, often including reference to instrumental accompaniment or musical forms.

The Bible in song
The course has shown us that expressing scripture in song should embrace a diversity of musical style and genre. Plainsong and Anglican chant provide direct settings of biblical prose; metrical hymns take a different approach; and other songs take biblical texts and expand them. Within this repertoire, we see narrative theology at work.

Music used creatively

Music is generally seen as the servant of text, but it is also a language in its own right, with the power to reach places that words do not. Music can encompass a remarkable richness and diversity which can both connect with us mere mortals and at the same time transport us from the ordinary and earthly towards the divine and heavenly. Music can also be used to minister love and compassion to others with gentleness. David ministered in music to Saul whenever he was afflicted by an evil spirit, whereupon he was soothed and calmed (1 Samuel 16.23). Seen most obviously in a funeral, music is frequently the trigger for tears. Tears during worship may also be a sign of God at work within those exploring faith.

The sound of sheer silence

Silence deserves a mention here, not least because it is as vital in worship as it is rare. Music makes no sense without notes of different length, rests and pauses; it requires rhythm, pace and flow. Psalm 46.10 encourages us to 'be still and know that I am God.' And Elijah found God not in the earthquake, wind or fire, but in the sound of sheer silence (1 Kings 19.12). God only spoke when all other 'noise' ceased. We may find silence unnerving, but increasingly there is a need for quiet space in a busy, noisy world. True worship and prayer belong as much to the silence as to the song.

Mission-shaped worship for nurture and discipleship

Christian song should always point us to God, aiding Christian formation. Luther put music on a par with preaching as a vehicle for proclamation of the gospel, nurture and discipleship. Others go further, arguing that what is sung is more likely to be formative for Christian faith and spirituality than what is preached, because of the way music engages both the head and the emotions, and aids memory. As we worship, we learn more about who God is and how to worship in Spirit and truth through judicious choices and an openness to transformation by God from one degree of glory to another (2 Corinthians 3.18).

Inspiring music in worship today

Jesus reminded his disciples that a wise teacher will bring out treasures old and new from the storeroom to further the kingdom of heaven (Matthew 13.52). The new does not replace the old but builds upon it. This is particularly true in a changing, mixed economy church with an openness to fresh vision and different ways of worshipping. Music cannot be consigned to the margins, but nor should it be the centre of what we do – it is a means to an end. Inspiring music in worship is not a simple linear pathway, but a spiral developing and deepening our experience as it propels us towards our final heavenly destination.

Some people have made a lifetime study of the theology of music. There is so much more to explore. The suggestions for further reading overleaf are a good place to start.

Further reading

Begbie, J. *Voicing Creation's Praise: Towards a Theology of the Arts* (T & T Clark, 1991)

Begbie, J. *Theology, Music and Time* (Cambridge University Press, 2000)

Begbie, J. *Resounding Truth: Christian Wisdom in the World of Music* (SPCK, 2008)

Bent, H. & Tipple, L. *Worship 4 Today, A Course for Worship Leaders and Musicians*, Parts 1–3 (CHP, 2013–14)

Bell, J. *The Singing Thing: A Case for Congregational Song* (Wild Goose, 2000)

Bell, J. *The Singing Thing Too: Enabling Congregations to Sing* (Wild Goose, 2007)

Dowley, T. *Christian Music: A Global History* (Lion, 2011)

Drake, N. J. *A Deeper Note: The 'Informal' Theology of Contemporary Sung Worship* (Grove Books, 2014)

Dudley-Smith, T. *A Functional Art: Reflections of a Hymn Writer* (Oxford University Press, 2017)

Ellis, C. J. *Gathering: A Theology and Spirituality of Worship in Free Church Tradition* Chapter 8 (SCM, 2004)

Ellis, C. J. *Approaching God: A Guide for Worship Leaders and Worshippers* Chapters 10 and 11 (Canterbury Press, 2009)

Hargreaves, S. & S. *Whole Life Worship: Empowering Disciples for the Frontline* (Inter-Varsity Press, 2017)

Harrison, A. *Recovering the Lord's Song: Getting Sung Scripture Back into Worship* (Grove Books, 2009)

Harrison, A. *Sing it Again: The Place of Short Songs in Worship* (Grove Books, 2003)

Jones, R., Routley, A. & Pollard, H. *Worship Works: A Workbook for Groups, Choirs and Congregations* (Christian Music Ministries, 2013)

Kroeker, C., ed. *Music in Christian Worship: At the Service of the Liturgy* (Liturgical Press, 2005)

Leach, J. *Thirty Ways to Use Music in Worship* (Grove Books, 2011)

Lomax, T. *Creating Missional Worship: Fusing Context and Tradition* (CHP, 2015)

Marks, A., ed. *How to use Voice for Life: A Choir Trainer's Guide* (RSCM, 2015)

Marks, A., ed. *The Voice for Life Guide to Choir Training* (RSCM, 2018)

Page, N. *And Now Let's Move into a Time of Nonsense: Why Worship Songs are Failing the Church* (Authentic Media, 2004)

Ward, P. *Selling Worship: How what we Sing has Changed the Church* (Paternoster, 2005)

Wilson Dickson, A. *A Brief History of Christian Music: From Biblical Times to the Present* (Lion, 1997)

www.rscm.com/IMiW contains supplementary online resources for *Inspiring Music in Worship*.

The Royal School of Church Music

The RSCM provides a huge range of resources and training, particularly through its education and publishing departments. These include:

- *Voice for Life* – a comprehensive scheme to support and promote singing in church and school

- *Church Music Skills* – training programmes for organists, cantors and music leaders

- *Lift Up your Voice* – a scheme for churches with few or no musical resources

- *Strengthen for Service* – for worship leaders, ordained and lay, and musicians

In addition the RSCM provides: training for music groups and ensembles; instrumental workshops; choral courses for young people; specialist organists' training; residential singing breaks; and local music and training events.

RSCM publications and resources include:

- *Church Music Quarterly* (CMQ) – theological perspectives, information, news and views

- *Sunday by Sunday* – a lectionary-based weekly service and liturgy planner

- *The Network* – information about locally organised events and courses

MusicDirect – the RSCM's on-line shop, with more than 2000 titles of printed anthems, services and organ music (e-mail: musicdirect@rscm.com)

Visit **www.rscm.com** for full details about the RSCM. At **www.rscm.com/IMiW** you will find access to all the supplementary on-line resources for this book.

Praxis

Praxis is the partner organisation working with the RSCM to support ministerial training across the church. Formed in 1990, Praxis is a national organisation sponsored by the Liturgical Commission of the Church of England, the Alcuin Club, and the Group for Renewal of Worship. Praxis offers practical guidance, inspiration and training to enrich and inform the practice of worship. Through its seven regional committees, Praxis provides opportunities in which different worshipping traditions of the Church can meet and engage creatively with one another. Visit **www.praxisworship.org.uk** to find out more.

Praxis News of Worship is a quarterly magazine with news, articles, book reviews and events relating to worship, liturgy and music.